CHRIST'S CHURCH
Evangelical, Catholic, and Reformed

Christ's Church

Evangelical, Catholic, and Reformed

73872

by

B<small>ELA</small> V<small>ASSADY</small>

Professor of Systematic Theology
Lancaster Theological Seminary

W<small>M</small>. B. E<small>ERDMANS</small> P<small>UBLISHING</small> C<small>OMPANY</small>
G<small>RAND</small> R<small>APIDS</small>, M<small>ICHIGAN</small>

Contents

Foreword

The question of the churches' response to the ecumenical imperative has been posed afresh to our generation. The primary reason is a deepened concern for the unity of Christ's Church and a desire to be obedient to His will that "there shall be one fold, and one shepherd." Christians of varied traditions now read together the New Testament with its repeated emphasis on the oneness of the Church and are convinced that the quest for unity is not optional. Moreover, there is a growing refusal to remain content with some vague spiritual unity which our competing denominational structures betray.

But there are other factors involved which add urgency to the quest for unity today. One is the situation among the younger churches, only recently freed from being denominational missions and still exhibiting the fragmentation which we have imposed upon them. They are restive, and understandably so, with our divisions being perpetuated among them. Another factor is the plight of the church at home, preoccupied with outmoded structures, introverted, stalemated in her mission, and reluctant to move with and ahead of the gigantic revolution that is transforming society all over the globe. Still another factor is the growing conviction that the response which the past generation made to the ecumenical imperative is no longer adequate or viable for us.

The response of the past generation to Christ's prayer "that they all may be one" was cooperative Christianity. It produced in the conciliar movement councils of churches at every level, ranging from towns and cities to states and nations, until finally the movement was climaxed by the formation of the World Council of Churches in 1948. These councils have made extraordinary achievements during the past half century. They have brought communions out of isolation, facilitated cooperative programs of life and work, provided a forum for discussion and increased mutual understanding, and in many cases have been instruments in the renewal of the Church. Today, however, there is a growing conviction that cooperation is not enough. It does not overcome the scandal of division within Christ's Church, nor does it remove the obstacle to mission which this division erects. Is it possible, many are asking, that the conciliar structures are an honorable but outmoded response to the ecumenical imperative, and that we are being summoned today to a more costly response, to the death of the forms of institutions which we have known and to the resurrection of forms that are still to be disclosed?

These questions provide the background for understanding unity negotiations that are taking place throughout the world. A new leadership has developed, men who are not lonely prophets isolated from their constituencies, but farseeing ecclesiastical leaders who realize that unity will not come without cost and that a part of this cost will be repentance.

One such leader is the Reverend Dr. Eugene Carson

Blake, whose sermon preached in Grace Cathedral in San Francisco late in 1960 inspired the movement now called the Consultation on Church Union. His was a bold proposal, aimed at nothing less than the reshaping of American Protestantism. Now six communions have come together officially to explore the possibility of establishing a united church, truly catholic, truly reformed, and truly evangelical. They are bound together in a common commitment to seek God's will for His Church today and to strive to be open and receptive to whatever God will say or do to make His Church a more effective instrument of His glory.

From the beginning it has been hoped that Dr. Blake's proposal would stimulate wide theological reflection and criticism, for what is being proposed is not simply a merger of institutions but a union of churches that are committed to the truth as it is revealed in Jesus Christ. One of the first to see the necessity of such criticism was Professor Bela Vassady of Lancaster Theological Seminary. In a series of closely reasoned chapters he has analyzed the idea of a Church that is catholic, reformed, and evangelical. To this task he has brought a rich background. Educated in his native Hungary, where he achieved a distinguished academic career, he was forced by the turn of political events to continue his vocation in America, where he had done postgraduate work as a young man. In both Hungary and the United States he has been actively engaged in the ecumenical movement, and his ecclesiastical membership now is in a communion, the United Church of Christ, that has been created by the coming together of four different traditions.

While Professor Vassady writes as a Reformed theologian, he leaves no doubt about his ecumenical commitment. His volume is a rich and valuable contribution to the ongoing discussions in the Consultation on Church

Union and to the quest for the unity and fullness of Christ's Church. It is to be commended to all those who seek a better understanding of the unity which God wills and His children seek.

JAMES I. McCORD

Introduction

By and large there are two main types of introduction. The first announces the central theme of the book and outlines the various subtheses to be covered in the sequence of its chapters. Such an introduction is usually prepared *before* all the other chapters are written. The second type unveils certain facts concerning the origin of the book and the history of its making; how it developed into the form of a book; how it received its title; what is (and is not) covered in it; and what should be regarded as its controlling perspective.

The first type of introduction has been used in my previous book *Light Against Darkness,* the second is employed here and now.

A LITTLE HISTORY

On December 4, 1960, Eugene C. Blake, the Stated Clerk of the General Assembly of The United Presbyterian Church in the United States of America, preached a sermon in Grace Cathedral, at San Francisco, California. The sermon outlined a proposal for the reunion of

11

Christ's Church. The 173rd General Assembly of The United Presbyterian Church in May 1961, upon the overture of some sixty Presbyteries, adopted the report of its Standing Committee in regard to Mr. Blake's proposal and extended an invitation to The Protestant Episcopal Church to join with The United Presbyterian Church in an invitation to The Methodist Church and The United Church of Christ "to explore the establishment of a united church truly Catholic, truly Reformed, and truly Evangelical." The Protestant Episcopal Church, meeting in General Convention at Detroit in September 1961, accepted the invitation. The response of The Methodist Church and The United Church of Christ was also favorable. Later on the International Convention of Christian Churches (Disciples of Christ) and The Evangelical United Brethren Church joined the first four Churches as full participants in what has since been called the Consultation on Church Union.

Thus far the Consultation has held three meetings. The first, an organizational meeting, was held at Washington, D.C., in April 1962. The second meeting (Oberlin, Ohio, March 1963) produced a surprising consensus on how decisions should be reached in a united church on questions of both belief and practice. The third (Princeton, N.J., April 1964) approved three statements on "One Ministry," "One Baptism," and "One Table." It is hoped that these will serve as an encouraging basis for the work that lies before the Consultation. The same meeting recognized that the establishment of an ordained ministry is critical to any union effort and decided to engage the members of the Consultation, with the co-operation of competent authorities in the field, in a serious study of "the ordained ministry in the united church," and of the ways by which it might be established. The fourth meeting of the Consultation is scheduled for April 1965, at Lexington, Kentucky.

THE BOOK IN THE MAKING

Ever since 1925 (the year in which the Stockholm Conference on Life and Work was held), I have been deeply interested in the church union movements. When I read Mr. Blake's San Francisco sermon, I immediately sensed that, as the years rolled by, slowly but surely it would have a remarkable reshaping effect upon the whole life of American Protestantism.

In the second half of 1961 I decided to devote three editorial articles in *Theology and Life* to a discussion of the central theological theme of the Blake proposal: What are the essential implications of the threefold concern that the forthcoming united church should be truly catholic, truly reformed, and truly evangelical? By the time I finished the writing of the first article, I realized that the number of editorials would have to be increased to at least five. And when I came to the fourth article, I was convinced that the vital issue of the divine-human continuity in the life of the Church (serving as a context for the problem of the "one ordained ministry") is bound to play a dominant role in the discussions on church union. For that reason I devoted three articles to this issue. And so the series of editorials gradually grew from three to eight and were published in volumes 5-7 (1962-1964) of *Theology and Life*. These, somewhat revised, now comprise the eight chapters of this book.*

When I began the writing of the first article (the first

* The publisher of this book wishes to thank the publishers and editors of *Theology and Life* for permission to reprint that portion of the material which first appeared in *Theology and Life*.

chapter in the book), the date and place of the first meeting of the Consultation on Church Union were not yet set and the First Session of the Vatican Council was nearly a year away. On the other hand, the eighth article in the series was finished before the third meeting of the Consultation at Princeton, N.J., in April 1964, and just before the Second Session of the Vatican Council closed in December 1963. By the time this book is published, the Third Session of the Vatican Council will have convened in Rome and the members of the Consultation on Church Union will be getting ready for their fourth meeting at Lexington, Kentucky. At that meeting, as well as in all forthcoming union conversations, most of the issues covered in this book will have to be faced and treated with clarity and charity. Otherwise we shall not be able to establish a united church truly catholic, truly reformed, and truly evangelical.

THE TITLE IN THE MAKING

The gradual shaping of the title of the book is also not without some relevancy. In his San Francisco sermon Mr. Blake used only the two adjectives "catholic" and "reformed," stressing that "a reunited Church must be both reformed and catholic." A few months later the General Assembly of The United Presbyterian Church added "evangelical" and initiated the exploration of the establishment of a united church truly catholic, truly reformed, and truly evangelical. These three adjectives are still being used, in the same order, by the Consultation on Church Union. The original series of articles published in *Theology and Life* changed this order by placing the "evangelical" *before* "reformed." The logic for doing so was that no church can be "truly reformed" unless the principles of its self-criticism and renewal are again and again rediscovered in the gospel (*evangel*) of Jesus Christ.

In the title of this book the reader now finds a third ordering: "evangelical," "catholic," "reformed."

By placing the adjective "catholic" in the middle we certainly do not wish to degrade it to a second place in relevancy. We simply wish to indicate that the catholicity of the Church is not to be identified with a set of doctrines and a system of truth; nor with a hierarchical status and a specific order in the Church. It is a dynamic reality and can be described only in paradoxical terms.

That church is catholic which does not dare to speak of its own nature without seriously considering also its mission; nor of its mission without an equal emphasis upon the givenness of its unique nature. In other words, the catholicity of the Church is both a gift and a task. As a gift, it is rooted and grounded in the gospel of Jesus Christ and in the Church's positive reponse to the same. Therefore it is *evangelical* through and through. On the other hand, it is also a task to be constantly undertaken, not only through the evangelization of the whole world but also (and primarily) through submitting the whole life of the Church to a continuously undergoing re-formation into the one permanent image of its own historic existence, which is Jesus Christ Himself. Therefore the catholicity of the Church is a *re-formed* and a *re-forming* catholicity.

The Objective

The purpose of this book is rather modest. It does not wish to give a detailed description of the life of the Church in a united form. It only wants to offer a certain theological grounding for any thinking about this most urgent question. And it would like to engrave into the minds and hearts of all Christians at each place one basic thesis: the three terms "evangelical," "catholic," and "reformed" are correlative and interdependent, and for that

15

reason should never be used in contradistinction to each other, nor should they be employed to indicate confessional or denominational belonging. All three point beyond the Church to its Head and Lord, and by doing that they become decisive aspects of the same one Church. They should never have been employed as party labels. Bishop Newbigin has expressed the same thing recently and so succinctly:

> When we use the words *catholic, reformed,* and *evangelical* as party labels, we are in danger of making them into servants of denominationalism. In fact, rightly understood, they are, all three of them, a summons to acknowledge that there is One who is sovereign over all denominations.[1]

The Controlling Perspective

Finally, the one controlling perspective that prevails in this book is that of the gracious relationship that exists between Christ and His Church, here described in terms of five key words: "control," "continuity," "concern," "contrition," and "commitment." These words point to the fullness, freedom, finality, and faithfulness of Christ, and guide the Church in being truly evangelical, truly catholic, and truly reformed.

All the dimensions of Christian unity, its height and length, its breadth and depth, can rightly be appraised only in the controlling perspective of this gracious relationship. Whether we are engaged with our relationships to local, national, or world-wide councils; or are invited to participate in interconfessional conversations and in consultations on church union; or involved in the

[1] Lesslie Newbigin, "Catholic, Reformed, Evangelical . . . What Do They Really Mean?" in *Presbyterian Life,* Vol. 17, No. 11 (June 1, 1964) , p. 34.

various relationships of local congregations, the most decisive issue remains always the same: both as individuals and as "churches" we must not cease to move on the high level of gracious relationship, where costly grace is responded to through costly discipleship and a *trialogue* is steadily going on between our gracious Father and our still divided churches. Otherwise our union negotiations would run into ever new dead-ends, and our so-called mergers would turn out to be but "cloaked reunions."

We surely shall get lost in the labyrinth of our varied "traditions"; we surely shall be found again and again in the midst of sheer *dialogues* on church orders and of endless "theologizings;" we surely shall be driven into a defensive position by the uniting forces of militant atheism and emasculating syncretism, unless we learn to conform ourselves to the basic order of the Creator Spirit: "Make a complete about-face and return again and again to the high level of gracious relationship. And make that complete about-face always *together,* so that as 'churches' you could become partners in repentance, partners in gratitude, partners in hope, love and obedience; in other words, partners in the gospel and under the power, guidance, and freedom of the Creator Spirit!"

In preparation for the New Delhi Assembly of the World Council of Churches, the writers of the pamphlet *Jesus Christ: The Light of the World* concisely and graphically summed up the ultimate goal of the ecumenical movement:

> It might be said that the World Council of Churches exists so that Christians around the world shall no longer speak of "they" and "we": "they" — the clergy, "we" — the laity; "they" — the men, "we" — the women; "they" — the Catholics, "we" — the Protestants; "they" — the old people, "we" — the young people; "they" of the East, and "we" of the West; "they — of the national church, "we" —

of the local congregation, or vice versa; but in obedience to Christ and in love and service of Him they may always and altogether say "we the Church of Christ."

How can we reach such a unity? Only through the path of sincere trialogues; through our searching and praying *together* for a united church truly evangelical, truly catholic, and truly reformed.

This small book was written to serve the cause of such a united effort.

CHAPTER ONE:

A United Church Truly Catholic

The word "catholic" is the translation of the Greek *katholikos*, meaning "throughout the whole" (world or universe). It stresses "general" in distinction from "particular," and "universal" in contrast with "limited." It points at things or traits that affect mankind as a whole and for that reason arouse a universal human interest. Today the epithet "catholic" is sometimes also used to describe (more or less boastingly) the open, cosmopolitan temperament of one's general attitude, comprehensive sympathies, and sophisticated tastes. Such a vague use of the word ("I am a man of catholic tastes!") differs completely from its ancient, ecclesiastical significance; however, our purpose is to expound the latter meaning.

CATHOLICITY MADE CAPTIVE

Alas, in our everyday language, especially since the period of the Counter Reformation, the ecclesiastical term "catholic" has become more and more a term of abuse. Its abuse is based on the incorrect assumption that "catholic" and "Roman Catholic" are interchangeable names. Roman Catholics are taught by their priests that the word "catholic" applies only to them but not to Protestants. And in a democratic society of multiple faiths, we all are more or less accustomed to speak, even if only for the sake of courtesy or brevity, of the Catholic (indicating the Roman Catholic), the Protestant, and the Jewish faiths. Such an uncritical use of the word "catholic" may, of course, easily prepare the way to a distorted image of Protestantism, namely, that Protestants are non-catholic or even anti-catholic, or at best represent but a diluted form of Catholicism.

A critical comparison of the meaning of "catholicity" as it was understood by the Church Fathers with that which it gradually assumed throughout the history of the Roman Catholic Church will, however, corroborate the conviction of the classic Protestant faith. On the one hand, the heritage and destiny of the Protestant churches can be understood and rightly appraised only in the historic context of Christian catholicity; on the other hand, Roman Catholicism, even though it departed from the original catholic faith, nevertheless has remained a historic form of the same catholicity. The best way to describe this form is to speak of it as catholicity made captive, or as a "cabin'd, cribb'd and confined" catholicity.[1]

Catholicity was gradually "cabin'd" as the emphasis laid on the primacy of the Roman patriarch (the pope) ushered in the centralization of ecclesiastical authority and finally led (in the eleventh century) to the separation between Western (Roman) Catholicism and Eastern

[1] The phrase in quotation marks is taken from Shakespeare, *Macbeth*, Act III, scene 4, line 24.

(Greek) Orthodoxy. It became more and more "cribb'd" as the Counter Reformation, climaxing in the doctrinal decrees of the Council of Trent, officially added to the "apostolic tradition" the "traditions" of the church as they developed through the centuries. And it became in a rather apodictic way "confined" when the Vatican Council of 1870 promulgated the dogma of the infallibility of the pope. The proclamation of the "Assumption of the Blessed Virgin Mary" on November 1, 1950, only placed one more seal upon this gradual process of confinement. The entire history of the Roman Catholic Church is a graphic demonstration of the fact that catholicity can become petrified in institutionalism and "encased within an ever hardening crust" (Tillich). It is utterly regrettable to see that the same church which in one of its authoritative documents, *Catechismus ad Parochos* (1566), so eloquently stressed that it does not let itself be "circumscribed within the limits of any kingdom, nor confined to the members of any one society of men but embraces within the amplitude of its love all mankind, whether Barbarians or Scythians, slaves or freemen, male or female," nevertheless through its Latinity, uniformity and juridically understood principle of hierarchy gradually imprisoned its own catholicity.

By whom and when can this captive catholicity be liberated? We believe that its liberation will have to come vertically from on high, that it will have to occur within the Roman Catholic Church itself, and that it will be affected, at least to a certain extent, in response to the beneficiary influence upon the whole Roman Catholic Church of the so-called ecumenical (reunion) movement. This movement bears out the evidence that in the Protestant churches there is again an increasing appreciation for the catholic aspects of the Church of Christ. The more we Protestants succeed in recapturing catholicity, the more hope there will be for the same catholicity to be liberated from its Roman confinement.

RECAPTURING CATHOLICITY

> The Reformers, in trying to recapture the wholeness and universality of the faith, were simply trying to be true "catholics."[2]

> Recent research on the Reformation entitles us to say that the Reformation began because the reformers were too catholic in the midst of a church that had forgotten its catholicity.[3]

> What Protestants can learn from the sixteenth-century Reformation is that *the catholic faith is recoverable*. It can break out of the strongest chains that men put around it.[4]

These and many similar statements that could easily be quoted from the writings of other contemporary Protestant theologians clearly indicate that in reference to catholicity "liberation," "recapture," and "recovery" are today the best possible words to be used. We must strive toward a United Church which is truly catholic. But our efforts will be successful only if we recover and recapture the original meaining of the word "catholicity" and try to liberate this concept from all unnecessary and ambiguous connotations which more and more shackled it in the course of many centuries. The Reformers endeavored to find their way back to the Church Fathers and to the primitive "apostolic tradition" witnessed to by the New Testament. By doing the same thing we shall come to the conclusion that the concept of catholicity is

---

2 Robert McAfee Brown, *The Spirit of Protestantism,* Oxford University Press, 1961, p. 19.

3 Jaroslav Pelikan, *The Riddle of Roman Catholicism,* Abingdon Press, 1959, p. 46.

4 Robert McAfee Brown, *op. cit.,* p. 20.

as manifold as the wisdom of God (Eph. 3:10). It has many facets and aspects, but they all converge in, or rather originate from, Him who is the Head of the Church and the Light of the world.

(1) *Catholic = universal.* The name "Catholic Church" occurs the first time in Ignatius' letter to the Smyrnaeans (c. 110) in the following sentence: "Where the bishop is present, there let the congregation gather, just as where Jesus Christ is, there is the Catholic Church."[5] The contrast here with the local congregation makes the meaning "universal" incontestably mandatory. But it would be utterly wrong to interpret this universality only in a quantitative, geographical sense. The reference to the presence of Jesus Christ makes its qualitative, theological interpretation unavoidable. Catholicity in the sense of universality gives the Church a dynamic character. It is rooted and grounded in the universality of the atonement of Christ.

St. Augustine in one of his later works, commenting on I John 2:2, says that Jesus Christ "is the propitiation of our sins," but he hastens to call the attention of his readers to the fact that John immediately added, "and not only of our sins, but of the sins of the whole world." "Think, brethren, what that means," he continues. "Surely, we are pointed to the Church in all nations, the Church throughout the whole world."[6] In another connection he stresses that there will always be need and room for the Church to grow in the world, and that Jesus did not promise that the Church would ever become catholic in a quantitative sense, i.e., that all men of all nations would or could ever be converted into believers. "Other-

[5] Cf. Cyril Charles Richardson (ed.), *Early Christian Fathers* (*The Library of Christian Classics*), Westminster Press, 1953, I, 115.
[6] St. Augustine, "Homilies on I John" in *Later Works* (*The Library of Christian Classics*), Westminster Press, VIII, 266.

wise," asks Augustine, "how shall that prophecy be ful-filled, 'Ye shall be hated by all for my name's sake,' unless among all nations are those who hate as well as those who are hated?"[7]

The Church then is catholic in the sense of universal because "God so loved the *world* that he gave his only Son for it"; because "God was in Christ reconciling the *world* to himself"; because the Lamb was slain and by His blood He did "ransom men for God from *every tribe* and *tongue* and *people* and *nation"*; and, finally, because Christ's missionary injunction, which is the driving force of the life of the Church at every place and in all ages, contains not only a universal promise but also a com-mission which is equally universal in its scope and pur-pose: "All authority in heaven and on earth has been given to me. Go therefore and make disciples of *all na-tions,"* and "You shall be my witnesses to the *end* of the earth."

The apostle Paul, whose earnest desire was to share in Christ's suffering while spreading the gospel, in his letter to the Colossians rejoicingly states: the gospel is bearing fruit and growing *in the whole world* (1:6). Whenever we confess our faith in "the holy catholic Church" we, too, should remember that the equation catholic = uni-versal can be rightly spelled out only in terms of the cost and joy of our own discipleship; and that this disciple-ship will always and everywhere have its world-wide (uni-versal) effects or at least implications.

(2) *Catholic = identical.* The first equation always indicates catholicity in space; this second equation, catho-licity in time. The name "Catholic Church" (*ecclesia catholica*) means that throughout its whole history the

7 St. Augustine, *Epistle CXCIX* in *Corpus Scriptorum Ecclesias-ticorum ·Latinorum,* LVII, 286-287.

Church cannot (and does not) alter its nature; it always remains identical with itself.[8] The basic question, of course, is: What guarantees this self-identity of the Church? One of the answers to this question establishes a third equation, catholic = orthodox, and a fourth, catholic = continuous.

(3) *Catholic = orthodox.* The equation catholic = orthodox began to present itself as soon as the Church encountered heretical teachings. Already in the second half of the second century the *Muratorian Canon* (c. 170) refers to certain views "which cannot be received in the Catholic Church, for gall cannot be mixed with honey." In most of the cases, however, the ideas of universality and orthodoxy occur together in patristic theology. Vincent of Lerins' famous maxim (c. 434) is a classic expression of the combination of the two equations catholic = universal, catholic = orthodox: "What all men have at all times and everywhere believed must be regarded as true." Of course, these and similar statements, if taken literally, would have made the definition of true Christian faith almost an impossible endeavor.

Precise definitions of the catholic faith were sought through the writing and approval of many ecclesiastical creeds, confessional books, and statements of faith. Alas, time and again these have been regarded not only as testimonies, but also as tests, of the orthodox catholic faith.

[8] Cf. Karl Barth, *Dogmatics in Outline*, Philosophical Library, 1949, p. 144. Jaroslav Pelikan (*op. cit.*, pp. 21ff.) describes catholic Christianity as "identity plus universality." By "identity" he means that which distinguishes the Church from the world — its message, its uniqueness, its particularity. By "universality," on the other hand, he means "that which impels the Church to embrace nothing less than all mankind in its vision and in its appeal." He demonstrates how the various elements of catholic Christianity (the missionary enterprise, church organization, church life, theology and the Church's *modus vivendi* with the state) involve some combination of identity and universality, but in different proportions.

A rigid and intolerant interpretation of the equation catholic = orthodox has often led (not only in the Roman Catholic Church but also in Protestant churches) to inquisitions, doctrinaire self-righteousness, and uncharitable censoriousness. The exclusiveness of catholic truth can be valid only in the inclusiveness of Christian love![9] For that reason, the catholic or orthodox faith can never be defined in quantitative terms. The revelation of God is not a system of truths. It is a Person. Ultimately, He alone (i.e., God in Christ), through His gospel and through the internal witness of His Spirit in our hearts and minds, can (and does) guarantee the orthodoxy of our catholic faith.

(4) *Catholic = continuous.* The same holds true also in the case of the equation: catholic = continuous.[10] To believe in the catholic Church means to believe in the continuity of Christ's work of salvation. The Church of Christ is one, holy, catholic, and apostolic, because Christ and His Spirit unchangeably use the same means of grace, i.e., the proclamation of the Word and the administration of the sacraments for the realization of men's salvation in and through the Church.

The so-called classic "marks" of the Church, its "oneness," "holiness," "catholicity," and "apostolicity," for this

9 Jaroslav Pelikan, *op. cit.,* p. 24, rightly observes: "Neither exclusive, nor inclusive alone, but catholic — such was the church that emerged from the missionary activity of the early Christians." If only it had always remained the same!

10 While Jaroslav Pelikan's short definition of catholic Christianity is "identity plus universality," the Swedish Lutheran theologian Gustaf Aulén regards universality and continuity as the two fundamental aspects of catholicity. "The two are closely related and cannot be separated. The church could not be the universal church if it did not through the ages stand in unbroken relationship with the original church which had its origin in Christ, the church of Easter and Pentecost" (*Reformation and Catholicity,* Muhlenberg Press, 1961, pp. 182ff.) .

very reason all belong together and cannot be separated. They are *syngenetic,* for they have their common rootage in the continuity of Christ's redeeming work. They are *synergetic,* as their efficacy can be experienced in the life of the Church only in their togetherness. Finally, they are *symbiotic,* as their intimate association is necessary to all of them. Each of them would wither without the others. The Church cannot be one without being holy; it cannot be holy without being catholic; and it cannot be catholic without being apostolic. Thus by stressing the apostolicity of the Church, we really point to its catholicity with reference to its visible, historic continuity. This, however, need not mean that we must locate the Church's catholicity in any one visible manifestation of its historic continuity. The latter always remains entirely dependent on the continuity and efficacy of God's eternal re-creative work in and through the Church. As Tertullian put it: "The Church is from the apostles, and the apostles from Christ, and Christ from God."[11]

Such an interpretation of the equation catholic = continuous stresses then the necessity of the apostolic ministry in the life of the Church; it even can and does propose that "the traditional threefold ministry in the apostolic succession be established in the reunited Church."[12] It cannot, however, in any case grant the possibility for any definite order (*ordo*) in the Church to claim infallibility for itself, especially not in regard to the administration of any of the means of grace. Whether it is called a papal, an episcopal, a presbyterian, or a congregational order, none of these can in itself be a guarantee

[11] Tertullian, "On Prescription against Heretics," 37, *The Ante-Nicene Fathers,* The Christian Literature Publishing Company, 1885, III, 261.

[12] Eugene C. Blake, *A Proposal Toward the Reunion of Christ's Church,* p. 9.

against heresy, or (to express the same in positive terms) a guarantee for the apostolic continuity of the Church. Such a guarantee depends entirely on Christ's twofold promise that He will be present in His Church until the end of this age, and that for this purpose He will continue to bestow upon us His Holy Spirit.[13]

At this point it will be enlightening to recall that the Lambeth Conference Report of 1958 (which was quoted by Bishop James A. Pike immediately following the sermon on Church Unity by Eugene Carson Blake) acknowledges the fact that God's redeeming work in Christ is not bound to the episcopal order. The Report states:

> We fully recognize that there are other forms of ministry than episcopacy in which have been revealed the gracious activity of God in the life of the universal Church. It is our longing that all the spiritual gifts and insights by which the particular Churches live to His glory may find their *full* scope and enrichment in a united Church.

The Report then goes on and emphasizes:

> The unity between Christian Churches ought to be a living unity in the love of Christ which is shown in *full* Christian fellowship and in mutual service . . . in free interchange of ministries, and *fulness* of sacramental Communion. Such unity, while marked by the bond of the historic episcopate, should always include congregational fellowship, active participation of both clergy and laity in the mission and government of the Church, and zeal for evangelism.
>
> Such is the vision we set before ourselves and our own people, calling them to regard the recovery and manifestation of the unity of the *whole* Church of Christ as a matter of the greatest urgency.

(5) *Catholicity = wholeness* or *fullness*. We have quoted the Report of the Lambeth Conference quite ex-

---

13 Cf. Gustav Aulén, *op. cit.*, p. 197.

tensively not only because of its reference to other forms of the ministry besides episcopacy, but also because in it the words "whole," "full," and "fullness" occur repeatedly. (These words in the quoted text of the Report were italicized by us.) Their use is symptomatic of the newest trend in the interpretation of the concept of catholicity and may be expressed in the simplest way by a new equation, catholicity = wholeness,[14] or fullness.

The roots of this interpretation can also be traced back to patristic theology (Cyril, Augustine, etc.), but primarily to the New Testament. Such contemporary theologians as the French Dominican Congar and the Dutch Reformed Hendrik Berkhof base their interpretations of catholicity in terms of fullness mainly on the epistles to the Colossians and Ephesians.

For Congar the catholicity of the Church is made possible by the fact that the Church is the place where the reality of unity is harmonized with the reality of diversity.[15] This harmonization unites the powers of cre-

[14] We quote here from two contemporary theologians who speak of catholicity in the sense of wholeness. Robert McAfee Brown (*op. cit.*, p. 19) writes: "The catholic faith is faith in its wholeness or totality. The catholic church is the church that proclaims the whole faith. And on these terms, the Reformers had no difficulty in affirming their belief in the holy catholic church and their allegiance to it. For them the issue of the Reformation was precisely the issue of catholicity." Lewis S. Mudge, in his Editorial Postscript to the conversation between theologians of the Reformed tradition (*Bulletin of the Department of Theology of the World Presbyterian Alliance*, 1961, vol. 2, No. 1, p. 15), makes the following comment: "Catholicity has to do with the wholeness of Christian faith and fellowship in time and space. Catholicity also points to the claim of the Gospel to have to do with the whole world in breadth and depth." One can readily observe that in these quotations the term "wholeness" really stands for a healthy combination of all the various equations surveyed in our discourse. The same holds true also of the term "fullness."

[15] Yves Congar, *Chrétiens Désunis, Principe d'un oecumenisme catholique,* Paris, 1937; English translation: *Divided Christendom,* by M. A. Bonsfield, London: Geoffrey Bles, 1939).

ation with the powers of redemption. The Roman Catholic Church is thus, according to Congar, a oneness in diversity, the "fullness of God" in operation, "a magnificent equilibrium of all aspects of truth," and it is through the Church that all things are re-created and fulfilled. This re-creation and fulfillment are not yet completed; they are still in the process of being worked out. The one-sided emphases of the separated brethren will have to be embodied in the life of the Church. In substance the Roman Catholic Church possesses all the necessary faith values. Partly because of the fact of separations, however, it still lacks the capacity to express its catholicity to the fullest possible degree. There must be, therefore, a mutual giving and receiving between it and the separated brethren. The latter again and again betray that they are stirred by "an authentic spiritual affection" toward catholicity, Congar asserts. Eventually they will return to the Catholic Church. In the meantime, they must be given all opportunity to meet with their "Catholic brethren."

Congar's views, which are regarded in the Roman Catholic Church as the hotbed of a "new theology" (*nouvelle théologie*), undoubtedly gave a sizeable impetus toward initiating Roman Catholic-Protestant dialogues primarily in Europe, but also in America. His emphasis upon the "fullness of God" in Christ and in the life of the Church gratifyingly paves the way to a return to the Scriptures and the Church Fathers. Nevertheless, Hendrik Berkhof is justified when he expresses his misgivings[16] in regard to Congar's teaching at least on three counts: (1) The customary Roman Catholic duality of nature and grace in this theology impairs the possibility of a Biblical understanding of catholicity. (2) Congar's emphasis on "all

---

16 Hendrik Berkhof, "The Catholicity of the Church" in *Bulletin of the Department of Theology of the World Presbyterian Alliance,* 1961, Vol. 2, No. 2, pp. 8-9.

aspects of truth," indeed, on "partial truths," and on "values," again indicates a quantitative interpretation of God's revelation and of our faith. (3) The image of organic growth does not adequately express God's concern with sinful man. In fact, no one image is adequate to describe our striving after catholicity in the sense of fullness. However, both the image of God's judgment and the image of His mercy, as they constantly qualify our striving, should by no means be neglected.

We conclude this section on recapturing catholicity with a short summary of Berkhof's views.[17] He acknowledges the partial validity of the classical quantitative understanding of catholicity: the Church will always have to break through its natural (geographical, social, political, racial) limits and boundaries. Such a breaking through, however, is possible only if the quantitative understanding of the Church is constantly subordinated to a qualitative understanding of its catholicity.

The point of departure in Berkhof's interpretation of catholicity is found in the Biblical image of "fullness" (*plēroma*). In the New Testament, the image of *plēroma* stands for the Person of God (Eph. 3:19) who permits the fullness of His deity to dwell in Christ (Col. 1:19; 2:9). The crucified and risen Lord has been made by Him "the head over all things for the church, which is his body, the fulness of him who fills all in all" (Eph. 1:22-23). Thus *plēroma* is primarily the gift of God to the whole world, in Christ and through His Church; but it is also a task set before us: "We are to grow up in every way into him who is the head, into Christ" (Eph. 4:15; cf. also Col. 2:19). It is our mandate to comprehend all the dimensions of the life of faith and love (Eph. 3:17-18) so that we "may be filled with all the fulness of God" (v. 19).

[17] Hendrik Berkhof, *op. cit.*, pp. 4ff.

This dialectic of gift and task indicates that the growth in catholicity is a growth in unity: "We grow from *plēroma* to *plēroma*," but this growth is possible only in the Church which is "understood to be perpetually on the way from potency to actualized fullness, from justification to sanctification." All this is the work of the Holy Spirit in us but it also "implies a certain structure as the peculiar instrument" through which this whole process of growth can be worked out. The various offices of the ministry are indispensable (Eph. 4:11-12); the proclamation of the Word puts the whole process in motion (Col. 1:5ff.) and also leads to its fulfillment (Col. 1:28); the call to "one faith, one baptism and one hope" (Eph. 4:4-5) is the driving power in the life of the members of the Church; but the ultimate good is nothing less than the bringing into unity (*anakephalaiosis*) of the whole world: in the "fullness of time" God's grand design will "unite all things in him [Christ], things in heaven and things on earth" (Eph. 1:10). For the same reason "the Christian congregation must learn to bring Christ into its daily life and to make the realization of his love the beginning of the *anakephalaiosis* of all things." And so, the catholicity of the Church, if it is truly, i.e., prophetically, interpreted as representing a day-by-day growing into the fullness of Christ, will have the widest and fullest possible foundation as well as consequences. It is not only founded in a sound witness to the God-man, i.e., in Christology, but in its teachings concerning the Holy Spirit and the Church it also assumes a dynamic character and significance, while at the same time it never ceases to point forward to its eschatological fulfillment.

TRULY CATHOLIC

What can we learn from this short, comprehensive survey of the various aspects and connotations of the terms "catholic" and "catholicity"? What do we mean when we say that the United Church should be truly catholic?

In answering these questions we shall use five basic words, all starting with the letter "c." They are: *control, continuity, concern, contrition,* and *commitment.*

The United Church will be truly catholic if it lets itself be *controlled* by nobody else but by Christ alone.

It will be truly catholic if it will derive its strength and life from the divine *continuity* of His redeeming work and will readily submit all the visible and historic forms of its ministry to His continuous judgment and mercy.

It will be truly catholic if it overcomes all ecclesiastical introversion, and by its witness, service, and unity makes evangelism and the missionary work of the Church its basic *concern.*

It will be truly catholic if it lives in constant *contrition* for all its sins and shortcomings.

And, finally, it will be truly catholic if its constant repentance drives it to make ever new *commitments.*

From all this one final conclusion necessarily follows: the United Church cannot become truly catholic without being truly evangelical and truly reformed. Our task is not simply to pray and work only for its catholicity, hoping that with it all the other things will be given to us. The first three basic words mentioned above, "control," "continuity," and "concern," point emphatically to the evangelical character of catholicity, while the last two, "contrition" and "commitment," clearly indicate its need for continuous self-criticism and renewal.

In other words, all the dimensions of the catholic faith, i.e., the height and length and breadth and depth of the catholicity of the Church, can be grasped only in their evangelical context and by pilgrims on the road of continuous reformation.

"Catholic," "evangelical," and "reformed" are correlative terms. If we have not learned at least that much from the history of the Church, we had better start learning it right away.

CHAPTER Two:

Truly Evangelical and Truly Reformed

The invitation extended by the United Presbyterian Church to other churches to participate in reunion discussions voiced not only the hope that the forthcoming united church would be "truly catholic" but also that it would qualify as "truly reformed and truly evangelical." We surmise that the order in this reference is due to the fact that the original Blake proposal spoke only of a church which should be "both reformed and catholic," and that the "evangelical" prerequisite was added to the first two only after it had been established that in Methodist circles this adjective would be much better understood. The logical and theological order, however, must necessarily place "evangelical" *before* "reformed." For no church can be "truly reformed" unless the principles of its reformation are constantly rediscovered in the gospel (*evangel*) of Jesus Christ.

"Evangelical" and "reformed" — how meaningful both

terms are; how rich in contents and how pregnant with dynamic connotations — they are worthy companions of that first term, "catholic"! Without them, our striving for catholicity would be but a vain and barren effort. The same holds true also with regard to the term "Protestant," which, if rightly interpreted, is a comprehensive term, embracing both the "evangelical" and the "reformed" aspects of true catholicity. Since one of the American churches invited to participate in the reunion conversations bears the adjective "Protestant" in its historic name, and since this is the church which, in its interpretation of catholicity, differs from the others, we find it advisable first to compare the comprehensive term "Protestant" with the term "catholic," and then to expound the richness and significance of the terms "evangelical" and "reformed," after the necessary conclusions have been drawn from this comparison.

"Protestant" Versus "Catholic"?

In ecumenical discussions it has become customary to speak of certain churches as representing the "Catholic tradition" and to contrast them with those which are of the "Protestant tradition." Three relevant historic references may suffice here as illustrative material.

The Amsterdam Report. In 1948, at the Amsterdam Assembly, the report on "The Universal Church in God's Design" frankly admitted that to differentiate between "Catholic" and "Protestant" traditions is but a "loose" way of describing both. Yet the same report continues to speak of "the emphasis usually called 'Catholic'" and contrasts it with "the one usually called 'Protestant.'" The first "contains a primary insistence upon the visible continuity of the Church in the apostolic succession of the episcopate," while "the other one primarily emphasizes the initiative of the Word of God and the response of faith, focused in the doctrine of justification *sola fide*." Then, in the immediately following two sentences, the report admits that "the first group also stresses faith, and the second also stresses continuity of the visible church in some form," and that "this difference of emphasis cuts across many of our confessional boundaries." But if that is really the prevailing situation in our churches, then would it not be better to cease describing our differences by a "loose" usage of the terms "Catholic" and "Protestant"? What is even more important, would it not be better to penetrate the theological and etymological depth of both terms, and to show that it is exactly in this dimension of depth that we might find the common origin of both? Of course, we cannot expect an ecumenical assembly to do this work for us. But there is hope that such a depth understanding will gradually emerge in the continuing reunion conversations between our churches.

The Report of Anglican Evangelicals. Our second reference is to the Church of England. In 1947, at the invitation of the archbishop of Canterbury, a group of Anglo-Catholic scholars summarized their findings with regard to the characteristic traits of the catholicity of their church in a document entitled *Catholicity*. A few years later, in 1951, a group of Anglican evangelicals, also at the invitation of the archbishop, wrote an irenic report on the same subject under the title *The Fulness of Christ: The Church's Growth into Catholicity*. The latter has a relevancy to the subject under discussion here.

The Anglican evangelicals clearly saw and stated that the "Protestant" claims to be truly "catholic" in the proper sense of that word. On the other hand, the "Catholic" also is a "Protestant" in the true sense.

> Protestantism is testimony on behalf of the catholic faith against uncatholic perversions of it. The opposite of

37

protestant is not catholic but perverted or un-biblical. The "catholic" likewise, in claiming to stand for the wholeness of truth, claims to be a protestant in the true sense. He bears his testimony to the whole truth against partial and lopsided versions of it. The opposite of catholic is not "protestant" but one-sided or sectarian.

This is certainly clear talk. Nevertheless in their report the Anglican evangelicals did not prove to be daring enough to draw the logical and methodological conclusion from their clear vision. They thought that "for the sake of clarity" they should rather follow the "somewhat cumbrous expedient" of the Amsterdam Assembly, and use the words "Catholic" and "Protestant" in the same "loose" (and that means, etymologically and theologically, inaccurate) way as they are usually employed whenever the respective traditions of the non-Reformation and the Reformation churches are the subject of conversation. To calm their conscience, throughout the whole report they printed the words "catholic" and "protestant" in inverted commas and without capitals whenever they were so used. They had to admit, however, the awkwardness of this device, hoping that its "very clumsiness may serve to draw attention to a serious lack in our modern theological terminology."

The Blake Sermon. If the Anglican evangelical divines, in their long report, did not dare to eliminate the customary use of the terms "catholic" and "protestant," then who could have expected such a thing to be done in one short sermon, preached by a Presbyterian minister in an Episcopal cathedral, that contained also a proposal toward the reunion of Christ's Church? Here, of course, I am referring to Eugene C. Blake's San Francisco sermon, which served as an initiating event for the presently ongoing conversations.

In his sermon Dr. Blake used the phrase "catholic parts

of the church." As soon as he uttered it, however, he himself must have felt that theologically as well as semantically it was a rather inaccurate phrase. The Church is either catholic in all its parts or it is not catholic at all. Nevertheless, Dr. Blake had to use this or any other similar phrase in order to indicate what he meant by the adjective "catholic." He did not mean "Roman Catholic"; nor did he mean "the holy catholic Church" of the Apostles' Creed. He used the term in the same "third sense" in which it is usually employed, specifically in "Anglo-Catholic or High-Church practices and understandings" of the Anglican and, for that matter, also of the Protestant Episcopal Church. But as soon as one uses the term in this "third sense" one is obliged to do so for the sake of contrasting it with "Protestant practices and understandings."

The Blake sermon, however, did not stop at such a contrasting. Its aim was to propose the establishment of a Church which would unite the "Catholic" and "Protestant" elements in an even broader and deeper way than that already present in the Protestant Episcopal Church. In his proposal Dr. Blake, of course, could not demonstrate that the true catholicity of the Church and the act of genuine Christian protesting are mutually and inseparably correlated. The former indicates its basic Christian "status" or being, while the latter serves as the essential as well as existential mode of its manifestation. All this will have to unfold itself — gradually but unavoidably — in the forthcoming ecumenical conversations between the churches. Three things may then become increasingly apparent: (1) To be a Christian means to be a catholic. (2) To be a Christian, and therefore a catholic, means to voice one's sincere protestations on behalf of the true catholicity of the Church. (3) The

Church, which in this way proves to be truly catholic, is at the same time truly evangelical and truly reformed.

THE CHRISTIAN: A CATHOLIC

In 1928, Pope Pius XI, in response to the world-wide interest aroused by the Life and Work Conference held at Stockholm in 1925, issued his so-called *Mortalium animos* encyclical. In it he again laid down the Roman Catholic conditions for a true religious unity within Christendom, and gave his reasons why the Holy See was not willing to participate officially in the ecumenical conferences of other Christian churches. He called those who convoked and attended such gatherings by two names: "pan-Christians" (*panchristiani*) and "acatholics" (*acatholici*). We wonder whether the present pope would still find it appropriate to resort to the usage of the first of these terms in the same way as Pope Pius XI did. In his *Mortalium animos* encyclical *panchristiani* was meant in a latitudinarian sense: the "pan-Christians" do not lag in proclaiming Christ and the necessity of a fraternal communion in Him, but regarding doctrine and church government they betray that they are "acatholics," not wishing to submit themselves to the one, infallible authority of Christ's sole earthly vicar, the Roman pope.

Pan-Christians — what a wonderful name that would make if it were not meant in the scornful way Pius XI used it. That is why the archbishop of Uppsala, Nathan Söderblom, did not hesitate for one moment gracefully to accept it on behalf of all who participated in the Stockholm Conference. But he interpreted it as meaning *Ganz-Christen,* complete Christians, fully or wholly Christ-like. At the same time Emerich Revesz, a Hungarian church historian, called attention to the fact that Paul in Colossians 3:11 speaks about the all-integrating effect of Jesus Christ in whom there can be neither Greek nor Jew, neither circumcised nor uncircumcised, neither slave nor free man (and, one could add: neither Roman Catholic nor non-Roman Catholic), because *panta kai en pasin Christos:* Christ is all and in all. And Winfred Monod, a French theological professor, pointed out that the opposite to "Catholic" is not "pan-Christian" but "pan-Roman." The Roman pope himself is "acatholic" to the same degree as he is "pan-Roman." We, however, are "catholics" for the simple reason that we endeavor to be "pan-Christians," that is, like unto Christ in everything.

Here is the place to mention that Martin Luther at one time felt inclined to substitute the word "Christian" for the word "catholic," affirming his faith in the "one holy Christian Church"; and that the old historian, Eusebius, once reported of an early Christian saint, martyred for Christ's sake, as having made repeatedly but one simple confession: "I am a Christian." This he repeated without alluding to any name, city, race, or anything else; "and no other word did the heathen hear from his lips." Because they were both Christians, Martin Luther and that old martyred saint were certainly also "catholics," members of the one Holy Catholic Church which is the body of Christ.

CATHOLICITY: GIFT AND COMMITMENT

All this points to one basic, primary fact: Jesus Christ Himself is the sole, permanent, catholic reality in the life of His Church, and therefore also in the life of each one of us as members of His Body. "Where Christ is, there is the catholic Church." And we can add, "Where Christ is, there are the catholics." If catholicity ever needed to be described in terms of a "new status" we would hasten to assert: There is but one catholic status-giver, and that is God Himself in Jesus Christ and through His Holy Spirit.

41

Catholicity, however, is something more than merely a status for which one can formally apply. It is a gift that must continually be received and a commitment that must ever be made again. And it is in this paradoxical way that we must speak not only of the catholicity of the Church, but also of the catholicity of the faith of each individual member of the Church.

The Church is catholic first of all in the objective-vertical sense, because it is Jesus Christ Himself who lives, speaks, and acts in its life. As "the earthly-historical form of the existence of Jesus Christ" (Barth), it is the *ecclesia catholica,* remaining always and everywhere one and the same Church. Rooted and grounded in Him alone, who is its Head, the Church thus receives its permanent identity again and again with the fullness of Christ which is freely given it, but which must also be freely received by it.

This act of receiving calls our attention to the second, subjective-horizontal, aspect of catholicity. For the catholicity of the Church is not something that floats above our heads and hearts. It can become actual only in the life of individual believers who, by virtue of their catholic faith — and that also means by virtue of their own commitments — are incorporated into His Body as living members thereof. At the same time, however, they are also constantly nourished, strengthened, and edified by the faith of their brethren. As Christians, we are therefore all people of catholic faith. A short depth analysis of this faith will show that whenever it is genuine it proves to be a multifunctional and a multidimensional point-event.

THE CHRISTIAN OR CATHOLIC FAITH

The Christian or catholic faith is first of all a *"point-event";* that is, it always involves the possibility, as well as the necessity, of choosing. The word "point" here indicates the concreteness and actuality of the event. As our faith develops in the realm of palpable experiences, its fulfillment is always represented by a culminating point, a consummation of past experiences. But the point again serves as a new point of departure, as a spiritual gateway to a new beginning. It can never be merely a resting point, as it will always point beyond itself to Him who alone is the catholic Truth (*veritas catholica*) and the Source as well as the End of our catholic way of life.

Such a catholic faith, furthermore, will have to be a whole-life reponse, a *multifunctional* point-event. Christ's love is "so amazing, so divine" that it "demands our soul, our life, our all." That is why the apostle Paul could not wish the Thessalonians anything better than such a complete or catholic mobilization of their whole self and life by God Himself: "May the God of peace himself sanctify you *wholly;* and may your spirit and soul and body be kept sound and blameless at the coming of our Lord Jesus Christ" (I Thess. 5:23).

Last, but not least, the Christian or catholic faith is always a *multidimensional* point-event. Its dimension of height is determined by the fullness of Christ, demanding from us complete obedience. Its dimension of length reminds us again and again of the freedom of Christ: that we should be thankful for His free yet continuous presence with us in the past, and hopeful with regard to the equally free yet certain uniting of all things in Him at the end. Its dimension of breadth sets before us the finality of Christ and constrains us to radiate His love toward all men. Finally, its dimension of depth calls to our attention the faithfulness of Christ, evoking in us repentance and a continual renewal.

It is a grand privilege and an equally great responsibility to *be* a person of catholic faith. But "being" in this instance really means being in the dynamic sense of "walking," and walking in the equally dynamic sense of "protesting." We cannot live the life of catholic faith without its concrete manifestation in and through the comprehensive act of "protesting." As Christians we must be *protesting* catholics.

THE CHRISTIAN: A PROTESTING CATHOLIC

The essence of a reality and the mode of its self-expression cannot be separated. Whatever holds true of the former must also be stated about the latter. For that reason the same two things must be reiterated here, even if in a new context: (1) The recapturing of the original meaning of catholicity is not possible without a recapturing of the original meaning of its mode of expression, namely, our protesting attitude. (2) Not only the catholicity of the Church (and our faith) but also our protesting must be described in paradoxical terms, that is, in terms of gifts and commitment.

The English word "protest" is derived from the Latin verb *protestari*. This Latin verb belongs to the group of the so-called *verba deponentia*, verbs which, though passive in their form, nevertheless lay aside their proper passive significance and assume an active meaning. Thus the active or affirmative meaning of the Latin *protestari* is "to testify," "to declare in public," "to bear witness." It is virtually composed of two other words: the adverb *pro-*, meaning "for," and the verb *testari*, "to be a witness." He who protests testifies *on behalf* of something or someone, witnesses *to* something or *for* somebody. The act of protesting is therefore primarily a positive-affirmative act. Its negative consequence, the negation of that which stands in opposition to what is affirmed, simply grows out from that first, positive affirmation. It is a logically unavoidable by-product. Therefore it should never be given an independent role. Whenever this occurs, the act of protesting (in the first, affirmative sense of the word) has already been replaced by the act of contesting, and he who still calls himself a Protestant has long been deformed into a "contestant" or "contra-testant."

There must be many such negative "Protestants" in our midst, people who find their delight in an attitude of sheer over-againstness, in mere negations. Otherwise a man like T. S. Eliot would never have dared to write: "The life of Protestantism depends on the survival of that against which it protests."[1] Nor would it have become customary among the people of Greece to apply two different words whenever they speak of Protestants. One of these words is the participle form of a verb used three times by Paul in his farewell address to the Ephesian elders (Acts 20:21, 23-24). The Greek *diamarturomenos* indicates one who testifies *of* or *to* something. It certainly is a positive-affirmative word. When, however, Greeks speak derisively of a Protestant as one who takes his delight in negative revolting, they simply allude to him as being a *protestantes,* one who displays the attitude of sheer over-againstness.[2]

However, simply because there are men among us who with their negativistic attitude render a disservice to the primarily positive term "Protestant," we should not feel compelled to stop using the verb "protest" in a way which is worthy of its inherent duality, that is, both in its affirmative and in its negative sense. But we must always be on our guard that the latter remain subordinated to the former, the negative to the affirmative, and never vice

[1] T. S. Eliot, *Notes Toward the Definition of Culture,* Harcourt, 1948, p. 75.

[2] I received this useful information from Dr. N. Nissiotis, Associated Director of the Ecumenical Institute, Bossey, Switzerland.

versa. At this point one basic theological consideration will come to our help.

Throughout the whole Bible God reveals Himself as His own witness. This self-testimony is primarily one unique self-affirmation: "I am the Lord your God." But with this affirmation is unavoidably coupled His word of prohibition: "You shall have no other gods before me."

The same duality prevails in all His words. Thus, for example, the call God gave to young Jeremiah committed him both "to pluck up and to break down" (that is, to protest against the evils of his own day) as well as "to build and to plant" (that is, to bear a positive witness to God's promise for the future). St. Paul, too, while confessing that the weapons of his warfare were not worldly, stressed that he was given *divine* power to do two things (cf. II Cor. 10:3-6) : (1) to take every thought captive to obey Christ (and this he did by protesting for the truth, i.e., for Christ, and thus discharging the ministry of reconciliation) ; and (2) to destroy arguments and every proud obstacle to the knowledge of God (this having been accomplished by his ministry of protesting against). And it was always through this same protesting for (which proved to be also a protesting against attitude) that the true Christians of all ages were enabled "to turn the world upside down" yet at the same time "to hold the world together."

It is genuine Christian experience that this twofold act of protest is God's gift to us. The crucified and risen Lord reminded His disciples that before they could become His witnesses they had to receive the power of the Holy Spirit. Paul, too, acknowledged: "No one can say 'Jesus is Lord' except by the Holy Spirit." And recently Wilhelm Stählin has called to our attention the fact that the Latin word *testis*, which is the noun form of *testari*, meaning "witness," ultimately derives from the word *testiculus*, indicating the male genital gland, the testicle.[3] A genuine Christian will always joyfully acknowledge that whenever he performs the twofold act of protesting for and protesting against, he is really used as an active agent of God's begetting (re-creating) will. There is no true protesting without an awareness of this holy inevitability (cf. I Cor. 9:16b and Acts 4:20). It can also be described as a liberating captivity.

But we have to discern also the other, the ethical, side of the same act. It is characteristic of the paradox of grace that no gift of God is offered to us without the commission that it be translated into the daily acts of our daily life. For that reason our protesting *for* and protesting *against* must become the permanent "style" of our everyday Christian living. Let us demonstrate this in regard to the issue that concerns us here, namely, the catholicity of the Church and our personal faith.

It is not enough to give only an intellectual assent to the fullness, freedom, finality, and faithfulness of Christ. For our catholic faith needs attestation. And there is plenty of opportunity for this as we encounter, in the "theatre of conflict" (Barth), both within and without the ecclesiastical fence, the anticatholic enemies of Christ's Church.

Such an attestation of our catholic faith demands the total mobilization of all its dimensions.[4] In the dimension of height our obedient witnessing (or protesting) *to* the fullness of Christ must be coupled with an equally obedient witnessing (or protesting) *against* all who try to tempt us to disloyalty to Him. In the dimension of

---

[3] Wilhelm Stählin, "Katholizität, Protestantismus und Katholizismus," in *Die Katholizität der Kirche,* edited by Hans Asmussen and Wilhelm Stählin, Evangelische Verlagswerk, Stuttgart, 1957.

[4] For a more detailed treatise of what follows, see the author's book, *Light Against Darkness,* Christian Education Press, Philadelphia, 1961, pp. 81-108.

length our protesting attitude must be motivated by *gratitude* for His free presence with us in the past and by *hope* based on this fact with regard to the future. And this gratitude and hope will also strengthen us in resisting all who try to curtail His sovereign freedom. In the dimension of *breadth* we must protest for the *finality* of His love, and attest our faith through evangelism and mission, by acting and speaking the truth in the spirit of the same *love*. Finally, in the dimension of *depth,* we must witness (or protest) to His *faithfulness,* demanding *repentance* and *renewal* first of all in our selves, but then also the radical transformation of all *status quo* worshippers.

The life of a genuine protesting catholic is indeed a full-fledged life. Such a life can be lived only in an evangelical context by one who steadily keeps on moving on the road of a continuous reformation. A protesting catholic is necessarily both an evangelical and a reformed Christian, as his whole life is embedded in a Church which proves to be truly catholic by being truly evangelical and truly reformed.

"Evangelical" and "Reformed"

A comprehenisve history of the terms "evangelical" and "reformed" still needs to be written.[5] Three things, however, can be ascertained about them. (1) During or immediately after the Reformation period neither of these terms was used antithetically to "catholic." (2) Both were and are employed quite often as synonyms. (3) To-

---

5 Very useful source material can be found in the following books and articles: H. Heppe, *Ursprung und Geschichte der Bezeichnungen, "reformierte" und "lutherische Kirche,"* 1859; Ernest Wolf, *Peregrinatio: Studien zur reformatorischen Theologie zum Kirchen-problem,* Kaiser Verlag, München, 1954; Wilhelm Niesel, *Was heiszt reformiert?* Kaiser Verlag, München, 1934. The historical references mentioned in this section are borrowed mostly from the writings of Heppe and Wolf.

gether they render a good service in expressing both the affirmative and the negative aspects of the act of protesting and in making us aware of its highly paradoxical nature.

The creeds and confessions of the sixteenth century speak of the one holy catholic and apostolic Church. Throughout the entire century we sense that the followers of Luther had a definite dislike for being called "Lutheran." Luther himself spoke out emphatically against those who labelled his teaching "Lutheran doctrine." He reminded everybody that it was neither the pope nor Luther who died for them, but Jesus Christ. Therefore they should call themselves and their doctrine by the simple name "Christian" or "Evangelical." The Apology of the Augsburg Confession complained, "The precious holy Gospel, they call Lutheran!" The seventeenth-century theologians M. Hoe and J. Gerhard endeavored to give an exposition of "the pure catholic-evangelical doctrine." And local congregations at most places called themselves simply the Christian or the Evangelical Church. The name "Lutheran Church" was accepted only later on to distinguish it from the churches that accepted, under Zwingli's and Calvin's influence, the so-called "Reformed" teaching or tradition.

Before the term "Reformed" could have assumed a confessional or denominational denotation, however, it had already been freely used by the new Reformation churches in Germany. Thus in the introduction to the Formula of Concord the Lutherans speak of their churches as "our reformed churches." One often comes across such phrases as *ecclesia reformata* (the reformed church), *ecclesia emendata* (the corrected church), *ecclesia repurgata* (the purified church). Lambert of Avignon, in his famous Homberg Articles of Debate (*Paradoxa*) already in 1526 urged: "All things should be reformed as far as they are

deformed." (*Omnia reformanda, qua deformata sunt*).
Even in the seventeenth century a theologian like Calixt
still used the name "Reformed" as a synonym for "Lutheran" and "Evangelical." In 1690 the two princes of
Braunschweig referred to the entire Evangelical (Lutheran) Church as being an "Evangelical Reformed Church."
Then there was a period when the Lutheran churches
stressed that not the Calvinistic but their own churches
were the "truly Reformed Church." Contrariwise, the
churches following the Calvinist tradition began to call
themselves "Reformed-Evangelical." By thus reversing the
order of the two adjectives, they wanted to indicate that
they alone were able to carry out the reformation completely. Finally the *Unions-Conclusum* in 1722 courageously denounced all confessional and sectarian name-call-
ing, and declared to favor the usage of two terms "Evangelical" and/or "Evangelical Reformed." By the latter
term they wanted to indicate that the Church is re-formed
according to the Word (or evangel) of God.

The terms "evangelical" and "reformed" should never
have been used in contradistinction to each other. Nor
should they ever have been employed to indicate confessional or denominational characteristics. They both represent basic, dynamic principles and for that reason are
correlative with the term "catholic."

Now, we have seen that the catholicity of the Church
(and of our faith) as well as its mode of manifestation —
the twofold act of protest — are both a divine gift and a
human task. But whence could we have learned all this,
if not from the gospel (evangel)? Therefore, the catholic
Church cannot live by anything else but by its loyalty to
the gospel. It can be truly catholic only by being truly
evangelical, that is, by its constant protesting for the
gospel, the whole gospel, and nothing but the gospel.

Since, however, such a witnessing (or protesting) *for*

the evangel is not possible without also witnessing (or protesting) *against* all things that are still deformed in the life of the Church, the Church can remain truly catholic only if it is willing to apply the principles of creative, prophetic criticism first of all to its own worldliness, arrogance, self-righteousness, and complacency. Thus, the truly catholic Church must also be a truly reformed Church, a Church that is aware of the fact that it can remain identical with itself only by continuously undergoing a re-formation into the one permanent image of its own historical existence, which is Jesus Christ Himself.

St. Augustine, in his commentary on the Psalms, while speaking of the Church, says: "Do you want to please [God]? You cannot so long as you are deformed. Let your deformity first displease you, then you will receive beauty from Him. For He will be your reformer who has formed you" (*Ipse enim erit reformator tuus, qui fuit formator tuus*) .[6]

God alone, in Jesus Christ and through His Holy Spirit, is the Former and Reformer of His Church. Are we really so displeased with our disunity that we are ready to receive His "beauty" in the form of a United Church, a Church which is truly evangelical, truly catholic, and truly reformed?

[6] Augustine, *Enarrationes in Psalmos,* Ps. 103, 5. 1, 4 (in: *Corpus Christianorum,* AO, 1476) .

CHAPTER THREE:

A Christ-Controlled Church

The United Church will be truly evangelical, truly catholic, and truly reformed if it is controlled by Christ alone. For that reason, the height *of our faith must be determined by the* fullness *of Christ as it demands from us complete obedience. That in turn means that our obedient witnessing (or protesting) to His fullness must be coupled with an equally obedient witnessing (or protesting) against everything that may tempt us to disloyalty to Him.*

WHO OWNS THE CHURCH?

The one, ultimately decisive act (and fact) in the life of each church is the kind of answer it gives, both in words and in deeds, to this basic question, Who *owns* the Church?

Howard Schomer, on his way back from New Delhi,

was welcomed in an Eastern Orthodox church of Moscow by the presiding bishop with the following words: "We have learned that the World Council of Churches, like the holy Church itself, belongs to nobody but to the Lord. And so we are very happy to belong with you to this world-wide fellowship in Christ." Schomer felt that the words of the bishop, freely translated into our own language, had great suggestive power. *"Churches that nobody owns" can be only those that are owned by Christ alone.* Such churches have no earthly proprietors. They are able to loosen every inherited bond of servitude and to liberate themselves from the state, from social classes, from ethnic groups, from protectors of traditions, from defenders of ideologies and cultures, in short, from all those whom they at the same time, in the very deep (Christian) sense of the word, must *serve*.[1]

The word "own" has at least two different meanings. Its primary meaning is "to possess." But the verb "own" may also mean "to acknowledge," or "to confess." Significantly, it is used in this secondary sense in one of the most ancient Christian hymns from the third century:

> *Hail, gladdening Light,*
> *..*
> *Holiest of holies, Jesus Christ, our Lord!*
> *..*
> *Son of our God, Giver of Life, alone:*
> *Therefore in all the world*
> *Thy glories, Lord, they own.*

The verb "own," when applied to the Christ-Church relationship in this twofold meaningfulness, has indeed much to say to us. On the one hand, it is Christ who

[1] Cf. Howard Schomer, "The Churches That Nobody Owns: Ecumenical Dynamics after New Delhi," in *Theology and Life,* Vol. 5, No. 2, pp. 158–169.

owns, i.e., possesses, the Church by controlling it. On the other hand, it is the Church which *owns,* i.e., acknowledges, Christ whenever in words and in deeds it *confesses* Him. And so Christ's control becomes manifest in the life of a *confessing* Church.

The content of this confession remains always the same. "Jesus is Lord!" — these were the words of the earliest and simplest Christian confession. "What is your only comfort, in life and in death? That I belong — body and soul, in life and in death — not to myself but to my faithful Savior, Jesus Christ" — thus read the first question and answer of the Heidelberg Catechism. And when applied to the Christ-Church relationship, the same confession finds its twentieth-century variation in these words: "The Church takes her life from this alone: she is daily and anew called, carried, comforted and controlled by her own Lord."[2]

It is this calling, carrying, comforting and controlling work of Christ that steadily informs the height of our faith. Or, to say the same thing in other words, the height of our faith is always determined by the fullness of Christ and our ever new response to it in our acts of daily obedience.

THE FULLNESS OF CHRIST

A serious study of the Church begins at the point where the image of "fullness" (*plēroma*) is taken in apposition with the image of "body" (*soma*).[3] This is distinctively the case in Ephesians 1:17 and 22-23 where it is stated that "the God of our Lord Jesus Christ, the Father of glory . . . has made him [Jesus Christ] the head over all

---

2 The fifth of the so-called "Düsseldorfer Thesen" in *Reformierter Kirchenzeitung,* 1933, p. 162.

3 Cf. Anders Nygren, *Christ and His Church,* Westminster Press. 1956, p. 93.

things for the church, which is his body, the fullness of him who fills all in all." "It is here," writes Anders Nygren, "that one can say that this concept ["Body of Christ"] touches upon an identity between Christ and his Church. The Church is identical with the 'fullness of Christ.' To be 'in Christ' is the same as to be in the body of Christ, and this is identical with Christ's Church."[4]

But we had better be cautious and note that the oneness of Christ with the Church, even in Ephesians, is not simply a matter of direct identity but of relationship. The apposition of the images of "fullness" (*plēroma*) and "body" (*soma*) only *touches* upon the identity between Christ and His Church. But that does not mean that the Church is factually "co-terminous with Christ."[5] The Lord, indeed, *does* share His own "fullness" with the Church; but besides the indicative of this sharing in the Epistle to the Ephesians we also meet the imperative of "growing up in every way into him who is the head, into Christ" (4:15), and the demand of "attaining to mature manhood, to the measure of the stature of the fulness of Christ" (v. 13). In giving His "fullness" to the Church, Christ, "in a proleptic and exemplary way" (H. Berkhof), reveals His gracious Lordship to the whole world. At the same time, His control over the Church is never an act of coercion. He wants His people to be willing, and to make their commitments to Him with the full purpose of a new obedience. The reality and the life of a Christ-controlled Church can therefore be best described in the following three inseparable statements: (1) Christ *constitutes* the Church; ours is the task to *commune* with Him. (2) Christ *convokes* the Church; ours is the task to *congregate*

4 *Ibid.*

5 Cf. Gustaf Aulén, *Reformation and Catholicity*, Muhlenberg Press, 1961, p. 185.

in Him. (3) Christ *confirms* the Church; ours is the task to be *conformed* to Him.

Before elaborating on these three themes, first two preliminary considerations are in order. The first concerns the Triune God and His work for, in, and through the Church. Even though in the three statements above only Christ is mentioned as the one who constitutes, convokes and confirms the Church, that does not mean that the Father and the Holy Spirit have nothing to do with it. We believe in and reaffirm that the basic rule of the external operation of the Triune God is its *indivisibility.* (*Opera trinitatis ad extra indivisa sunt.*) The Church is the Church of "the God of our Lord Jesus Christ, the Father of glory." It is He who made Christ "the head over all things for the church." And while Christ is the "head of the church," the Holy Spirit is, as it were, its "soul," or we could also say its "heart" (*cor ecclesiae*). "The Holy Spirit is likened to the heart," wrote Thomas Aquinas, "since He invisibly quickens and unifies the Church."[6] God always works as Father, Son and Holy Spirit, and the various aspects of His mighty deeds should never be parceled out among His three modes of being. Thus when we speak of a Christ-controlled Church, we mean a Church which is called, carried, comforted and controlled by the Father, the Son, and the Holy Spirit. And whenever we stress the work of one of the three Persons specifically, the work of the other two is implied at the same time.

The second preliminary consideration has to do with the sort of reciprocity which uniquely characterizes the Christ-Church relationship. This reciprocity is well stressed by the *Lund Report of the Faith and Order Conference* (in 1952): "Christ is never without His Church; the

[6] Thomas Aquinas, *Summa Theologiae,* III q. 8 ad 3.

Church is never without Christ. Both belong inseparably together, the King and His people, the keystone and the temple, the Head and the Body." Bishop Nygren, too, affirms this, writing succinctly: "The Church cannot exist without Christ; Christ cannot be present without His Church. The Messianic people cannot exist without the Messiah; the Messiah cannot be a Messiah without a people. Thus they are mutually connected with the other, and this reciprocity is essential."[7]

It certainly is essential. Nevertheless, it must be noted (as Nygren, too, admits later in his book) that this "reciprocal, contingent relationship is of a wholly different sort."[8] May we put it in this way: it is a reciprocity with a hole in it — or should we rather say, with an open valve in it? But whether we use the image of a "hole" or that of a "valve," both are meant to represent the priority of God's movement in Christ for the Church as well as the openness of the Church and its members toward this divine initiative. "The primacy of the self-movement of God"[9] is present in the event of the incarnation and in the event of the atonement as well as in the origin and the continuing life of the Church. Therefore it is not at all satisfactory simply to say: "Christ and the Church are correlative: the one is never without the other."[10] For it must also be stated that in the Christ-Church relationship *Christ alone remains the controlling Subject.*

Nevertheless, we can also say that there is a correlation between Christ and His Church. This correlation, however, has its origin as well as its end in what can best be described as "correlation plus." The Church — if truly

---

[7] *Op. cit.,* p. 31.

[8] *Op. cit.,* p. 90.

[9] Claude Welch, *The Reality of the Church,* Scribner's, 1958, p. 98.

[10] Nygren, *op. cit.,* p. 92.

the Church — will always remain aware of the fact that the Lord is its "absolute owner," and the Church is but His dependent "subject" or "property." In other words, God in Christ and through the work of His Spirit never ceases to be the sovereign, controlling Lord of the Church. He is that wholly other, divine "plus." He is the One who makes the Church utterly dependent on Himself, yet at the same time, in the life of its members, allows it to enter in a relation of personal interdependence with Him.

But let us now expound the three basic assertions, one by one and in their inseparable correlation.

CHRIST CONSTITUTES THE CHURCH

Christ controls the Church first of all by virtue of the fact that He is the One who constitutes it. All other social entities come into being by certain people getting together and constituting themselves into a group, a conference, an association, or an institution. The *raison d'être* of the Church, however, lies in the fact that its members are constituted and incorporated into it by the fullness of Christ, their Lord.

The "fullness of Christ" here indicates His whole person: His deity as well as His manhood, His lordship as well as His servanthood. In Him God and man were (and are) unconfusedly, unchangeably, invisibly and inseparably united. And this oneness is manifested also in His act of constituting the Church.

"The love of Christ controls us," wrote Paul to the Corinthians. He meant primarily Christ's love for us, and only secondarily, as a response to it, our love for Him. Christ controls the Church by His *agapē*-love; by His own sacrificial living and sacrificial giving for the world. It was quite natural for an Epicurus to visualize *philia*-love (the love of tender emotion) as dancing around the *oikumenē* (the whole inhabited earth). *Agapē*-love, however, can never be pictured as such an easy-going love. It accomplished something entirely different. It assumed human flesh and bled for the world.

The fullness of Christ's self-giving was essential to *His* being God for us and of *His* being man for God as well as *His* being man for man. His identification with sinful humanity was not only God's act for man but also an act of Christ's true humanity for both God and man. The Church could never have become constituted without His assumption of our human nature in the mystery of the incarnation and without His taking our place and making Himself one with us in the equally great mystery of the atonement. His Lordship and servanthood are exhibited in both: His Lordship in His condescension, humiliation, suffering, and sacrifice; and His servanthood in His faith, gratitude, hope, and love, all directed towards God as He lived the life of obedience "unto death, even death on a cross."

Yet the fullness of His self-giving did not cease with the crucifixion. The risen Lord, who is at the same time the exalted servant, continues to identify Himself through the Spirit with us. He intercedes for us. He steadily incorporates us into His Body which is the Church, sharing His fullness again and again through the forgiveness of sins. His identification with sinful humanity is a universal self-offering, an offering for the whole man and for all man. And so, all those who believe in Him are constituted by Him into a universal, catholic Church which again points forward to the "fullness of time," the consummation of His Kingdom, the final uniting of all things in Him.

We Must Commune with Him

To Christ's act of constitution corresponds our act of communion with Him. Faith as a whole-man response, as a multifunctional and multidimensional point-event, finds its fulfillment internally in our "mystical union with Christ" (Calvin) but expresses itself also externally in the life and work of the Church as an ontologically ordered and historically founded community.

Our communion *(koinōnia)* with Christ is not to be interpreted as a status or institution. It always has the nature of an event. It is our dying and rising "with" Him both in our inner life and in our public churchmanship, so that we may also abide and live in Him.

In receiving the baptism of John, which was a "baptism of repentance for the remission of sins," Jesus, the only righteous One, vicariously identified Himself with us sinners, and set out on a path leading to His suffering and death as well as to His resurrection and ascension. In receiving *our* baptism, we are incorporated into His death and resurrection, and our whole life is opened up to a redemptive participation in His fullness from which alone can we receive grace upon grace (John 1:16).

Our communion with Him is thus the gateway to that "third dimension" (Barth) in which God's gracious deeds break into our life. In this new realm of redemption we are promised to become "partakers of the divine nature" (II Pet. 1:4), and our new humanity is reorientated and reconstituted around and in His true humanity. In it we find a new meaning for our own life as well as a purposefulness for the history of all mankind. All this, of course, can be perceived only by those who believe in Him; it remains hidden from the eyes of the world until the day of His final revelation. But wherever this communion with Him occurs, in response to His act of constitution, there, and there alone, is the Church as "the living community of the living Lord Jesus Christ in the fulfillment of its existence." [11]

11 Karl Barth, *Church Dogmatics* IV, 1, p. 652. See also his contribution to *Man's Disorder and God's Design* (The Amsterdam As-

One more thing needs to be mentioned here. Even though the Church as a unique community takes its origin from our communion with Christ, it is at the same time also our participation in the life of those who believe in Him. It is the "communion of saints," a fellowship wherein each member exercises His spiritual gifts and shares them with the others so that all can and do learn from one another. It is a worshipping, witnessing, and serving community; an ontologically well-ordered and historically continuing Church.

The faith of this community always precedes the faith of those who are united in it; and the community itself has and maintains a priority over its members. This again is best expressed by the sacramental act of baptism. "We *are* baptized — it is something that is done to us, not something that we ourselves do. And what is done to us is that we are incorporated into Christ, so that we become His and are no longer our own."[12] He is the One who constitutes us into a Church; ours is the task of communing with Him, or to use the dynamic words of Martin Luther, the thing that behooves us is "to fall back again and again to our baptism," which is a baptism into His death and resurrection.

CHRIST CONVOKES THE CHURCH

Secondly, Christ controls the Church by virtue of the fact that He is the One who convokes it.

In the Statement of Faith of the United Church of Christ the verb "call" occurs twice. We confess that God "calls the world into being," and that the same God "calls

sembly Series), Harper and Brothers, 1955, on "The Church — the Living Congregation of the Living Lord Jesus Christ," pp. 67—76.
[12] "One Lord, One Baptism," in *Studies in Ministry and Worship*, No. 17, ed. by G. W. H. Lampe and David M. Paton, SCM Press, 1960, p. 57.

us into His Church." "Call," indeed, represents a commanding word. In it, we can almost hear the sound of a calling God echoed and re-echoed by the star-spangled recesses of a rapidly and yet so slowly expanding universe. And we can also hear that the same commanding word of God is addressed to each one of us personally but in such a way that we dare not treat this event as a "private affair." Christians prefer to speak of their "common calling."[13] We all "share in a heavenly call" (Heb. 3:1) and are members of the *ekklesia,* the Body of those who are called out of darkness into God's marvelous light.

"The Lord calls us through the Gospel," John Calvin emphasized, while Martin Luther used many verbs in order to describe the saving effects of this call: "The Church is conceived, fashioned, nurtured, born, reared, fed, clothed, graced, strengthened, armed, and preserved solely through the Gospel. In short, the entire life and being of the Church lie in the Word of God, as Christ says: 'By every word that proceeds from the mouth of God man lives.' "[14]

The Church can be truly evangelical, truly catholic, and truly reformed only if its whole being inheres in God's Word and nowhere else. This Word is primarily Jesus Christ, the incarnate Lord. In the Holy Scriptures we are encountered by the person of the same "speaking God" (Calvin). When the gospel is proclaimed, whether in the form of a sermon or in that of a simple testimony, again the same Word of God addresses us personally. Finally, when the sacraments are rightly administered and sincerely received, in a dramatic and tangible way God's same Word is made visible to our very eyes. The proclamation of the Word and the sacraments are "comple-

13 Cf. with the title of W. A. Visser't Hooft's book *The Pressure of Our Common Calling,* Doubleday, 1959.
14 *Luther's Works,* Weimar Edition, 7, 721.

mentary" though not "identical" modes of Christ's self-giving. The Anglican Evangelicals have expressed it correctly: "Where the sacraments are neglected the emphasis in worship tends to become exclusively individual, rational, and edificatory; while when the Word is neglected it tends to become exclusively corporate, sub-personal, and sacrificial. Each is needed to correct the other."[15]

Christ convokes His Church, that is, gathers, preserves and defends it by the fullness of His Gospel. But without the sacraments we could never speak of its fullness.

WE MUST CONGREGATE IN HIM

To Christ's act of convocation corresponds our act of congregation.

"To congregate" means "to assemble," "to come together," at the call of one who has the authority to extend a summons. The Church as a living community is *there,* and *only* there, where people who believe in Christ's all-controlling authority respond to His divine call and gather together to confess their faith in Him. The same John Calvin who asserted, "The Lord calls us through the Gospel," also hastened to add, "We who were called, respond in faith." The Church comes into being and is kept alive in this dual act of convocation and congregation. It is both God's act of covenanting with us and our covenant reponse to His commanding call. In this correlation-plus-act God's election is mysteriously carried out. By coming together *in Him* we learn that even though *we* responded to His call, yet ultimately *He* was the one who had chosen us and not we Him. The Church as a congregation is His chosen people.

Certain Church Fathers bore witness to this unique na-

15 *The Fulness of Christ: The Church's Growth into Catholicity,* p. 69.

ture of the Church by describing it as *tertium genus* ("the third race"). The same phrase is used also in contemporary theological conversations. The members of the primitive Church were chosen both from the Jews and the Greeks, yet they all became one in Christ Jesus (cf. I Cor. 12:13; Gal. 3:28; Col. 3:11). Thus the phrase denotes not only the supra-racial character of the Church but also its comprehensive oneness. God, by bestowing His Holy Spirit upon us, creates and renews the Church of Jesus Christ, "binding in covenant faithful people of all ages, tongues and races."[16] He does not take them out of this world. They can and, in fact, do remain citizens of their own respective countries and members of their own nations and races. Culturally and politically they may differ among themselves, but in their coming together in Christ they are one: "a chosen race," "a royal priesthood," "a holy nation." As there is but one Saviour, so there can be no more than one people of God. As there is but one divine call, so there can be no more than one congregation. The Church as "the third race," as a catholic congregation, is indivisible. But God meant this to be made visible — in the concrete worship, order, witness and service of each concrete local congregation.

Christ Confirms the Church

Thirdly, Christ controls the Church by virtue of the fact that He is the One who confirms it. This confirming work is threefold: it convicts, comforts, and counsels the Church. And it is transacted through the agency of the Holy Spirit.

In His work of conviction the Holy Spirit proves to be the only infallible examiner and at the same time a most

---

[16] Quoted from the Statement of Faith of the United Church of Christ.

inexorable and radical judge. His diagnosis begins with the Church; His judgment with God's own household (I Pet. 4:17). He always strikes on the right place, "reads each wound, each weakness clear," and says to us and the Church we are part of: "Thou ailest here and here!"[17] His infallible insight stems from His all-penetrating and all-unveiling light-nature, while His radical and inexorable judgment is prompted by His self-giving love. And what else could be more inexorable than *agape*-love?[18]

But it is exactly this love that couples mercy with His judgment and comfort with His work of convincing; for the Spirit of God not only convicts but also comforts the Church.

He comforts it by pouring God's love into our hearts, taking us into His possession, and dwelling in us; by knitting us together in a new fellowship, filling it with His righteousness, peace and joy, and endowing it with His many gifts; by cleansing and sanctifying His Church in granting us freedom from the flesh and the law, and opening before us a new and purposeful life; by commissioning and enabling us to be His witnesses, to serve as ministers of His new covenant, and to speak His truth with boldness and love. Last but not least, He comforts us also by interceding for His Church; by assuring us of our adoption as sons; and by serving as God's pledge and guarantee in our hearts.

Finally, Christ's confirmation includes also His steadily ongoing work of counseling. And this, too, is performed by Him through the Spirit.

Counseling is not an irrational thing; on the contrary,

---

[17] The quotations are taken from Matthew Arnold's "Memorial Verses." What he said here about Goethe can be stated truly and unreservedly only of Christ and the Spirit.

[18] For a detailed and enriching exposition of this thought see Donald M. Baillie, *God Was in Christ*, Scribner's 1948, p. 173.

it is rational through and through. God is willing to sit down and "reason together" with His people. His Spirit is always at hand, serving as a reasonable Counselor. And in this work of counseling He makes the best use of God's Word as His "vehicle" (Luther). There is "a kind of mutual bond" (Calvin) between the certainty of the Spirit and that of the Word. And this becomes manifest as He helps "the perfect religion of the Word" to abide in our hearts and minds[19] through His counseling operation.

To this counseling belongs first of all the mobilization of our memory. The Spirit brings to our remembrance all that Jesus once taught to His immediate disciples. If Christian education does its basic task of imparting the biblical truths and facts, the Holy Spirit will certainly always be at hand to enliven them in due time and to make them efficacious in our daily life. Without His inspiration, however, we would surely prove to be slow in our harkening back to the gospel. Without His illumination we would be unable to discern the mighty works of God and to understand the gifts He bestowed on us. It is the Spirit who helps us in searching everything, even the depths of God. He guides us into all the truth; He teaches us all things and gives us the *charisma* of interpretation. Spiritual authenticity in our sermons, audacity and genuineness in our witnessing, selflessness in our service and ministry — all these are prompted by the Spirit through His continuous work of counseling.

WE MUST BE CONFORMED TO HIM

To Christ's act of confirmation corresponds our act of being conformed to Him — or at least, it should do so. For "as God the Father has reconciled us to Himself in

19 Cf. John Calvin, *Institutes*, I, 9, 3.

Christ, so He has exhibited to us in Him [i.e., in Christ] a pattern, to which it is His will that we should be conformed."[20]

Conformity here means transformation to the likeness of Christ, actualization of the height of our faith, obedient witnessing (or protesting) to His fullness in words and in deeds, and an equally obedient witnessing (or protesting) against all who may tempt us to curtail His fullness in the life of the Church.

At this point it must be emphasized that the living members of the living Church of our living Lord must become aware of at least three relevant things: Firstly, that the fullness of Christ, offered to them in the life of the Church, is not only a gift but also a goal. It demands from them constant growth. It is "not a pillow, but a root which must bear fruit."[21] And since the fullness of Christ's self-giving was exhibited both in His Lordship and in His servanthood, the Church that wants to be conformed to Him must "imitate" the pattern He laid for it as its Servant Lord. Otherwise its growth into fullness will give place to "arrested development."

Secondly, the Church, just like its members, has an "ambiguous existence," and is conditioned by apparent "polarities," "contradictions," and "ambiguities."[22] It is at once sinner and sanctified. In its life we can meet not only an imitation of Christ but also a "rebellious rejection of the 'servant-form,'" and an "idolatrous desire for the 'lord-form.'"[23] Thus the Church needs a continual cleansing by Him who never ceases to constitute, convoke and

---

[20] John Calvin, *Institutes*, III, 6, 3 (Allen translation).
[21] Hendrik Berkhof, *The Catholicity of the Church*, p. 7.
[22] Cf. Claude Welch, *op. cit.*, p. 20; *One Lord, One Baptism*, pp. 26—27; Joseph Haroutunian, "The Reunion and Renewal of Christ's Church" in *McCormick Quarterly*, March 1962, pp. 38-41.
[23] Claude Welch, *op. cit.*, p. 123.

confirm His Church. Ours is the "shame," His alone the "glory," of the Church.

Thirdly, growing into the fullness of Christ's self-giving demands from the members of the Church a life of complete *obedience* — not a grudging obedience; nor one that is prompted by fear, enlightened self-interest, or rapid calculations; but a genuine, Christian obedience motivated by trust in Him and fraught with repentance, gratitude, love, and hope. Such an obedience will time and again cut across easily accepted dichotomies and deadlocks, choosing rather that "third way" (which is also the hard way) as it strives to avoid the identification of the gospel with this or that human ideology and courageously leads us beyond all human ideologies. It will always joyfully witness to His Lordship and resist all who might arrogate to themselves the right to rule the Church for Him. It will witness to the beauty and the spiritual richness of the "servant form," and strive to overcome any false pride, jealousy, or vain ambition in the life of the Church. Finally, it will be ready to accept, and daring enough to face, any crisis situation that may arise from such an obedient witnessing. It will share with Him the form of the suffering servanthood and remain loyal to Him to the end, knowing that in the life of an obedient Church the end proves to be but a new beginning.

Only such a conformity can be held as representative for a Church which is truly evangelical, truly catholic, and truly reformed. And it certainly is available to all the "churches." He who continuously constitutes, convokes, and confirms His Church cannot demand anything less than this from us. Ours is the task so to pray, so to witness, and so to serve that in the forthcoming United Church we may finally attain to it.

CHAPTER FOUR:

Divine-Human Continuity I

The United Church will be truly evangelical, truly catholic, and truly reformed, if it takes its life always and solely from Christ's continuing work of salvation. For that reason the length *of our faith must be determined by the* freedom *of Christ as it demands from us* gratitude *and* hope. *That in turn means that our witnessing (or protesting) to His freedom must be motivated by thankfulness for His presence with the Church in the past, and also by hope for His presence, with regard to the future. And as the length of our faith meets with the height of it, we are made participants in the movement of apostolic succession, which is the basic divine-human continuity in the life of the Church that underlies and informs everything else.*

CHRIST'S ONGOING WORK

Our first basic word was "control." The second is "continuity." A Church that is truly evangelical, truly catholic, and truly reformed will not regard itself either overtly or covertly as a self-perpetuating, self-propagating, and a self-propelled social entity. It simply cannot exist, not even for one second, without believing that its visible, historic, human continuity derives its origin as well as its perpetuity solely from Christ's ongoing work of salvation.

This work of Christ is always twofold. On the one hand, it transpires between the free movement of the Spirit and our direct encounter with it, here and now; on the other hand, it is also mediated and conveyed to us historically, through the continuing ministry of the Church. The former calls to our attention the *freedom* of Christ, the latter the role of the dimension of *length* in our Christian faith. And only by a constant subordination of the latter to the former shall we be able to develop and uphold a truly evangelical, truly catholic, and truly reformed doctrine of the apostolic succession.

THE FREEDOM OF CHRIST

The love of God revealed in Jesus Christ is not only "most full," it is also "most free."

> *O love of God most full,*
> *O love of God most free,*
> *Come warm my heart, come fill my soul,*
> *Come lead me unto Thee!*[1]

The "fullness of Christ" would not be complete without His "freedom." He is the Lord of the whole world and the Head of the whole Church in the fullness of His free-

[1] The first stanza of Oscar Clute's (1840-1901) hymn, *O Love of God most full . . . .*

70

dom and in the freedom of His fullness. To jump from the "fullness of Christ" to a doctrine of the "fullness of the Church," without paying due regard also to His freedom, has been one of the great temptations of many theologians throughout the centuries. This temptation can be overcome only by a consistent and constant stressing of the freedom of God's grace as it is continuously offered to the Church by the Father, in Jesus Christ, through the Holy Spirit.

The phrase "freedom of Christ" means at least three things. First of all, it indicates that the revelation of God in Christ and through the Spirit was, is, and ever shall remain God's free and sovereign act. Both in the life of the world and in the life of His Church He acts at all times as a free and sovereign Agent. He should never be identified with a "world process" or "consistent principle," nor with any ecclesiastical structuring. His Spirit is not "a legal, or technical, or symbolical It,"[2] but moves freely when and where He wills. There is no civil or ecclesiastical authority that can control Him or confine His presence and action. The freedom of God's Word is also the freedom of His Spirit, and until the day of final consummation the Spirit will always cause fresh light to break forth from His Holy Word. Martin Luther never ceased repeating: "We are asking for nothing more, nor have we ever asked for anything more, than the free Gospel."[3] Christ's freedom, just like His fullness, is made known to us only in His gospel, as it is freely offered, freely communicated, and freely received.

Secondly, the concept of the "freedom of Christ" means that, while on the one hand He is free to bind Himself to human instruments, fragile vessels, and concrete historical

---

[2] Karl Barth, cf. *Church Dogmatics,* IV, 1, p. 717.
[3] *Luther's Works,* Weimar Edition, 2, 341.

forms, yet on the other hand He never surrenders His sovereignty to any ecclesiastical office, liturgical form, or creedal formulations, but remains transcendent over all. He can, and indeed does, speak when and wherever He pleases, and the incalculability of His sovereign call to His ambassadors-in-the-making often takes us, both individually and corporately, by complete surprise. We should, for example, never forget that while His immediate disciples were deeply concerned with the proper criteria and the right procedure of filling the vacancy caused in their number by the betrayal and suicidal death of Judas Iscariot, the crucified and risen Lord was already preparing to call to the apostleship Saul as His "chosen vessel." He did not overrule the corporate, orderly decision of the eleven, and Matthias was duly enrolled with them as an apostle, yet by extending His sovereign call to Saul and by making him an apostle He demonstrated to all forthcoming generations that He was, and is, free to enlist in the apostolic ministry whomever He wants, and in His own specific way. Undoubtedly, there is and there must be a certain ordering in the ministry of the Church, otherwise the *laos* (people) of God would again and easily turn into a *chaos* (disorder) of sinful men, yet God will always reserve His own freedom over against any ecclesiastical order to show that His judgment does not necessarily agree with ours, and that our much cherished ways are not necessarily His. And so we must learn time and again "that God retains His freedom in His revelation and that the life of the Church, the Communion of Saints, is 'hid with Christ in God.' "[4]

Thirdly, the concept of the "freedom of Christ" necessarily postulates and, what is even more, also includes, the

[4] Daniel T. Jenkins, *The Nature of Catholicity,* Faber, 1942, p. 74.

freedom of the Church to respond to His sovereign call. God's binding Himself to us in Jesus Christ and His continued availability to us through the Spirit call forth a freedom and a binding also on the part of the Church as we voluntarily partake in His fullness and freedom through the act of faith.

This act, whenever it transpires in the members of the Church, proves to be a paradoxical and saving correspondence between "divine continuity" and "human discontinuity." On the one hand, it is possible only because there is an ongoing continuity in Christ's ministry to and in the Church. This work is uninterruptedly fulfilled through Him who (to use the words of Visser 't Hooft) is always "behind us, beside us and in front of us." Or as Deissman has put it, He is "about us on all sides." There is certainly no discontinuity in Him or in His deeds.

On the other hand, whenever, in the act of faith, He is apprehended by us, or rather we by Him, a radical discontinuity takes place in our human life. This is a "radical" but not a "complete" discontinuity since the change brought about in us by His free ministry does not suspend or destroy the identity of our selves. However, it brings forth the new state of a liberating captivity, the event of a radical transformation, the movement toward a revaluation of all values, a renewal of what is old, and a redeeming of what is present.

And so the Church, in and through this radical discontinuity, as it again and again occurs in the life and ministry of its members, is *continually* being surrendered into the hands of death, for Jesus' sake, so that the life of Jesus may also be manifested in its mortal body (cf. II Cor. 4:11).[5] Without the repeated experience of this continuous discontinuity, it could not remain a Church

[5] The translation here follows the New English Bible.

that is truly evangelical, truly catholic, and truly reformed; nor could it ever draw the joyous conclusion that
God's service, in response to Christ's free and full ministry, is indeed and always "perfect freedom."

THE DIMENSION OF LENGTH

All that has been said about the "freedom of Christ"
will serve to guard us against what we could call the "ma-
terialization" of His fullness. If the "fullness of Christ"
were something like a supernatural substance, then it
could be easily viewed in itself, isolated and detached from
everything else, and transmitted from one generation to
the next in a quasi-mechanical, impersonal way. But the
"fullness of Christ" is not a "thing" and not a "substance."
It can be known only in the free act of His self-giving
to each one of us and in our free and joyful response to
Him through the act of obedience. All this must be clear
to us after what has been stated concerning the dimension
of height in the act of faith.

Now we must go one step further, however. For just as
the "fullness of Christ" should never be separated from
His "freedom," so also the dimension of height in our
Christian faith may never be isolated but must always be
viewed together with all the other dimensions. At this
point it is our task to focus our attention primarily on
the dimension of *length,* since it is in and through this
dimension that we become fully aware of His sovereign
freedom.

The dimension of length in the life of faith always
stretches in two opposite directions. It has a backward
stretch, as it takes us into the unrepeatable past; and it
has an onward stretch, as it points toward the immediate
as well as the more remote future. On the one hand, it
brings to our attention the "fullness of time," as it oc-

curred at the midpoint of human history in the life, death, and resurrection of Jesus Christ; and it also makes us aware of the historic continuity of the Church, as we find ourselves "surrounded by so great a cloud of witnesses," by the company of faithful generations all of whom bore witness to His free presence with them in what we call "the past." On the other hand, it also helps us to anticipate His free presence with us in the near as well as in the more remote future as it ushers in once more the "fullness of time" in the event of His ultimate coming promised to us in the gospel. And we know that then and there we shall see Him as He is.

The backward stretch of the length of faith kindles in us the act of gratitude; the forward stretch, the act of hope. And so we learn that our faith, in response to Christ's free self-giving yesterday, today, and tomorrow, always works through gratitude as well as through hope. It is with their help that we are enlisted in the mighty army of the continuous succession of witnessing and serving believers.

FAITH'S BACKWARD STRETCH: GRATITUDE

There is a basic kinship between the New Testament words "grace" (*charis*), "gift" (*charisma*), and "gratitude" (*eucharistia*). The spiritual relevance of this kinship can be best demonstrated in the Church's continuing ministry.

The Church not only *has* a ministry, it is through and through ministry. Its essence in this respect can best be expressed as follows: The Church is the ministry of Jesus Christ. Three things are meant here.

(1) By giving Himself again and again through Word and sacraments, Jesus Christ serves the Church, and through the Church the whole world, uninterruptedly.

Grace and truth come to us in His continuing active ministry.

(2) This ministry of Jesus Christ is the gift of God's free grace to the whole Church. But it should never be viewed as something that is given to us in a lump. Since God's grace is inexhaustible and flexible, His ministry in and through the Church is offered to us in a variety of gifts. Each gift opens up a new possibility for service. The ministries of worship, vocation, and order (which are the three elemental forms of the Church's ministry[6]) may, and indeed do, assume many new forms in the life of the Church. There is, however, one common trait that binds them together: they all bear witness to God's repeated "condescension" to us, and to His ever new "adaptation" or "accommodation"[7] of Himself to our sinful human conditions.

(3) Christ's charismatic ministry to the Church evokes a free and responsible response in us and is reflected in our joyful service to Him. The hidden mainspring of this service is gratitude. Whatever form it takes, it is always our thank-offering to Him. We are humbled as well as elevated in knowing that to Him alone we owe that we are all ministers, members of His ministering Body, which is the Church. He made us free agents of His inbreaking Kingdom, fellow witnesses and fellow servants for Himself so that in sharing His abounding grace with more and more people "the greater may be the chorus of thanksgiving that ascends to the glory of God."[8]

The triumphant voice of this chorus is echoed and re-echoed in the pages of Church history. But only those can hear it who have learned to read those pages with a pro-

---

[6] Cf. Robert Clyde Johnson (editor), *The Church and Its Changing Ministry*, Philadelphia, 1961, pp. 14-25.

[7] Expression frequently found in John Calvin.

[8] II Cor. 4:15, NEB.

found gratitude for Christ's continuous presence and ministry in the life of His Church. For them the living apostolic witness is found everywhere: in the "high" as well in the "low" liturgies, in the ecumenical creeds as well as in the various confessions of faith, and in the diverging church policies and forms of governments. It is present in the "historic episcopate," in the "presbyterian order," and in the "church meeting" of the Congregationalists. It is found in the act of incorporation into the Body of Christ, in holy baptism, and in the *"continuance* of the Church"[9] made visible in the Lord's Supper, also called the eucharist, since it is an act of shared thanksgiving.

Viewed high from the plateau of gratitude the entire history of the Church turns out to be primarily Christ's story, the story of His continuing presence and ministry in the ongoing life of the Church. Only on that plateau can we learn how to be willing listeners to each other's "traditions," how to develop a new appreciation for the varying gifts embodied in them, and how to enter into a genuine dialogue with one another, prompted by nothing else but by the spirit of mutual thanksgiving. Last but not least, only on that plateau can we really learn how to be humble, how to put first things first, and how to be sincerely thankful for any progress in our united witness and service to the world.

Only a thankful Church knows how to participate in Christ's ministry, how to derive its continued existence daily from His grace alone. Paul's confession concerning his apostleship applies also to the entire life of the Church: By the grace of God I am what I am, and His grace toward me was not in vain. But even though I have worked hard throughout the centuries, yet it was not I

[9] Karl Barth, *The Knowledge of God and the Service of God*, Hodder and Stoughton, 1939, p. 195.

who did so but the grace of God which is with me (cf. I Cor. 15:10).

FAITH'S FORWARD STRETCH: HOPE

Genuine Christian gratitude never develops all by itself. It is always born together with and accompanied by genuine Christian hope. There is a mutual bond between the two: faith's backward stretch is reinforced by its forward stretch and vice versa. A grateful Church is at the same time a hopeful Churh, and a hopeful Church a grateful Church — thankful to Christ not only for what He did through the Church in the past but also for all that it hopes He will do for it in the unknown future. The Church's hope thus becomes a hope fraught with gratitude because its thankfulness was also fraught with hope.

There can be no sound doctrine of the Church without a sound eschatology. The adjectives "catholic," "evangelical," and "reformed" are also thoroughly eschatological terms and ought to be interpreted accordingly. The concept of "catholicity," whether taken in a quantitative or in a qualitative sense (the right procedure is to take it in both senses), will always remain a "boundary-line concept" (*Grenzbegriff*).[10] It indicates something that *is*, but also something toward which we are still heading; something present but also future; something we can only believe in and hope for. When used together with the adjective "evangelical," it clearly refers to the "wholeness" of the gospel and reminds us of the fact that there is no one communion on this earth that can be *fully* catholic because there is no one that is *fully* evangelical; for none of them is able to possess, in the full and absolute sense,

10 Cf. Wilhelm Stählin, *Katholizität, Protestantismus und Katholizismus*, pp. 190-191.

the "wholeness" of the gospel.[11] From all this necessarily follows the eschatological character also of the third adjective, "reformed." *Ecclesia reformata sed semper reformanda.* The Church is truly reformed by being again and again re-formed. And the completion of this reformation is not possible "until it is fulfilled in the kingdom of God" (Luke 22:16) .

The eschatological nature of the Church, its constant living not only in the act of gratitude but also in the act of hope, becomes even more conspicuous when we relate it to the one great "controlling category of biblical theology for both Old and New Testaments,"[12] namely, to the Kingdom of God. In this respect the admonishment of J. A. T. Robinson is very appropriate: "Just as the New Testament bids us have as high a doctrine of the ministry as we like, as long as our doctrine of the Church is higher, so it commands us have as high a doctrine of the Church as we may, provided our doctrine of the Kingdom is higher."[13] This demands at least four things: (1) The Church should never be viewed in itself, but must be related and subordinated to the Kingdom. (2) It should be looked upon as a means to an end and never as an end in itself. The Church is here for a purpose. That purpose, however, is God's "eternal purpose which he has realized in Christ Jesus our Lord": "that *through the Church* the manifold wisdom of God might now be made known" to the whole world (cf. Eph. 3:10-11) . (3) In its endeavor to fulfill this task the Church may not claim the lordship of the Kingdom for itself. "The task of the

[11] Cf. *The Catholicity of Protestantism* (R. Newton Flew and Rupert E. Davis, editors) , Philadelphia, 1950, p. 24.
[12] J. A. T. Robinson, "Kingdom, Church and Ministry" in *The Historic Episcopate in the Fullness of the Church,* edited by Kenneth M. Carey, Dacre Press, Westminster, 1954, p. 15.
[13] *Op. cit.,* p. 17.

Church is to preach the gospel to the world and to leave judgment to God; entrance into the glory of the Kingdom is not determined by the Church on the basis of an ecclesiastical McCarran-Walter immigration act."[14] (4) God's judgment, which is of course His gracious judgment pronounced in Jesus Christ, will always begin with His household, that is, the Church (cf. I Pet. 4:17); and only by continually undergoing the discipline of His *krisis* does the Church *become* a loyal agent for God and His inbreaking Kingdom.

This discipline of God's *krisis* in the life of the Church is effected by the threefold coming of the True Light into the world; and it can be understood only from the perspective of a threefold eschatology.[15]

The witness of the Church throughout the centuries points first of all to a *realized* eschatology, namely, that in Christ all the promises of God made in the Old Testament have been fulfilled. At the midpoint of human history the True Light has conquered the powers of darkness. It is true, the conflict between light and darkness is still going on and the Church remains till the end the Church Militant. Nevertheless it continuously derives new strength from the knowledge that the decisive battle has been won by God in Christ, and from discerning with a grateful heart "the signs," "the wonders," and "the mighty works" of God in its own ministry.

Secondly, the witness of the Church also opens up the perspective of a *futurist* (or *end-of-the-time*) eschatology. Anchoring its hope in the promise of the crucified and risen Lord, the Church looks forward with uplifted head

---

14 Claude Welch, *The Reality of the Church*, Scribner's, New York, 1958, p. 212.

15 For a more detailed discussion of what follows see the author's book, *Light Against Darkness*, Christian Education Press, Philadelphia, 1961, pp. 35-36, and Chap. 3.

to His ultimate coming when the victory of light over darkness will be made public to all men.

But neither of these two eschatologies could have a bearing upon the life of the Church here and now without a concern for the "eschatological present," the recognition of the saving significance of the "redemptive now": *"To-day,* when you hear his voice, do not harden your hearts" (Heb. 3:7, 15). *"Now* is the day of salvation" (II Cor. 6:2b). Now, "while it is still today" in the life of each member of the Church, the gratitude for the "Christ of the past" must meet the hope anchored in the "Christ of the future." And as these two meet and reinforce each other, every one of us will have to learn, in his own concrete situation, that we are ever dealing with the "Christ of the present." In other words, the realized and futurist eschatologies become relevant only through a *personal* or *immediate* eschatology. It could also be called *in actu* eschatology, indicating the continuous sequence of crisis situations in which we must die with Him again and again so that we also can live in Him and our faith can arouse us to ever new acts of gratitude and the equally new acts of hope. This is indeed the point at which we can realize that the Church "in all ages has her life and continuity in a marvelous preservation, in being constantly called out of death into life."[16] Only in the context of this marvelous divine preservation can the true meaning and role of apostolic succession be properly grasped and rightly interpreted in the life of the Church.

APOSTOLIC SUCCESSION

In the phrase "apostolic succession" both words are of equal importance.

---

[16] T. F. Torrance, *Conflict and Agreement in the Church,* Lutterworth Press, 1959, I, 62.

Succession means an uninterrupted series of persons or things that follow each other. There can be no succession without continuity in the sense of unbroken connection in time as well as in space. Without succession or continuity in the flux of events, human history could simply not last. It would necessarily come to an end.

The same holds true of the Church Militant. The reality of the Church, too, has its historic continuity. Church history, like human history in general, is a succession of events. In fact, it must never be viewed as isolated from world history. Not only is the Church in the world; the world, too, is in the Church. The events of both the Church and the world interlock. And so they must be kept, and interpreted, together.

Yet there is a distinctive qualitative difference between Church history and the history of the world. And the source, locus, and purpose of that difference can be defined only theologically. For they all point to God's gracious act in Jesus Christ for the world.

The historic existence and continuity of the Church would be meaningless without the fundamental theological claim that God has entered, and enters again and again, the arena of world history and there makes the historic continuity of the Church a continuous reality. Melanchthon, in defining the Church, has placed this basic theological claim in bold relief: *"Est enim ecclesia coetus non alligatus ad ordinarium successionem sed ad verbum Dei. Ibi renascitur ecclesia, ubi Deus restituit doctrinam et dat Spiritum Sanctum."*[17] Viewed horizontally, the Church is, indeed, only one society *(coetus)* among many others. It, too, is an association or community of people, but one with an unbroken historic continuity in time as

17 Melanchthon, *De ecclesia et de auctoritate verbi Dei* in *Corpus Reformatorum* (1539) , 22, 598.

well as in space. Yet this continuity can never be satis-
factorily explained merely in terms of an "ordinary succession." It points beyond the natural or immanent laws
of historical successions. For it always depends on God's
Word and on the recreating work of His Spirit.

It was the commission and the function of the apostles
to bear witness, in words and in deeds, to this fundamental theological claim and historic fact. And all those
who later on had the courage to do the same thing proved
to be their followers. They participated and still participate in the ongoing movement of apostolic succession.
"Christians trace their genealogy from the Lord Jesus
Christ" [18] but they do not bypass His first commissioned
witnesses, the apostles.

An apostle is one sent forth. In the absolute sense of
the word, Christ alone is Apostle, for He alone received
His apostolic mission directly from the Father. The Holy
Spirit is the personal Representative of both the Father
and the Son. He is the Apostle Spirit.[19] The first apostles
derived their apostolate historically from Jesus: "As the
Father has sent me, even so I send you" (John 20:21),
and supernaturally both from the Son and the Holy Spirit.
T. F. Torrance has summed this up succinctly: "The
Church on earth is founded historically upon the apostles
commissioned by Christ, but founded supernaturally by
the baptism of the Spirit sent by Christ at Pentecost; so
that the Church has a double relation to Christ, historically through the apostles, and supernaturally through
the Holy Spirit."[20]

When compared with all the other offices which developed in the primitive Church, the first apostles had a
special position. First of all they alone were the original

[18] The words of one of the early Apologists.
[19] Cf. T. F. Torrance, *op. cit.*, p. 24.
[20] *Ibid.*, pp. 24-25.

disciples. Their number was twelve, in strict correspond-ence with the historical twelve tribes of Israel. Thus they played the role of connecting link between the Old and the New Testaments. Then, too, they were the eyewitnesses of Jesus' death and resurrection. Thirdly, the message of which they were the *first* proclaimers was a *once-for-all* message that could be repeated but never changed.

After the death of the first apostles, in the nearly two-thousand-year history of the Church, nobody else could again spell out in his own person or office these distinctive marks of the original apostolate. No other officeholder in the history of the Church could claim to stand on the threshold between the Old and New Testaments, nor that he was an eyewitness of His resurrection, nor that he received the once-for-all message, historically speaking, direct from the Lord. And yet it is not only possible but theologically (and that means spiritually as well as his-torically) necessary to speak of apostolic succession in the life of the Church, for three reasons.

First of all, the divine commission to proclaim the gos-pel was not restricted to the first apostles. Their followers were bidden by them to remain witnesses of Jesus Christ in spite of the fact that they had not met Him in the flesh. They were told, however, to build their own witness upon the foundation laid down by the prophets and the apostles (Eph. 2:20). Thus they were not allowed to change the original message. Only in demonstrating their loyalty to the same gospel could they prove themselves true followers of the apostles, i.e., participants in the apostolic succession.

Secondly, the first apostles, as heralds of the resurrec-tion, were not simply preaching it as a fact; "they were living in it as in a new country."[21] And they looked upon

21 James S. Stewart, *A Faith to Proclaim*, Hodder and Stoughton, 1953, p. 109.

all forthcoming disciples and proclaimers of the same resurrection as full-fledged citizens of this "new country" and as "fellow heirs with Christ," whose dynamite was to be their own faith. "He who believes in the Son of God has the testimony in himself" (I John 5:10a). Thus by virtue of his faithful witness every Christian becomes contemporaneous with Christ, a link in the unbroken spiritual chain of apostolic succession. What he has heard from the first apostles or their loyal followers he will entrust to "faithful men." So through their individual witness they in turn transmit the message to others (II Tim. 2:2). The spark of witnessing thus springs from faith to faith and communicates God's eternal message through faith for faith (Rom. 1:17). And so the apostolic succession turns out to be in reality nothing else but "the succession of the faithful."

Thirdly, the apostles followed their Lord by unreservedly serving Him. But in so doing they have also rendered an inestimable service to the forthcoming generations. For they have laid an exemplary pattern before us all: their following (i.e., any legitimate apostolic succession) can be (and must be) spelled out only as a succession of service.[22] It is simply not possible just to "stand" in the apostolic succession. We must always walk in it, work in it, serve in it. And only by so doing can we also grow in it.

The Church could not be Church without this steadily ongoing movement of the apostolic succession. And this movement is not limited to any one part, section, level, or "order" in the Church. It is, and always must remain, a whole-Church movement, an external, visible manifestation of the innermost, invisible dimensions of our Christian faith. The "apostolicity" of the Church concretely and definitely indicates that in its life "height" meets

[22] Cf. Karl Barth, *Church Dogmatics*, IV, 1, pp. 718-720.

"length" and "length" meets "height"; obedience to the "fullness of Christ" as proclaimed by the apostles is coupled with gratitude for His free presence with them and their followers in the past history of the Church, but also with a hope for His free presence with us in the unknown future as the Church endeavors to fulfill its apostolic mission to the world.

A thankful and a hopeful obedience to the "whole" Christ and to the "free" Christ — a continuous dying *with* Him and living *in* Him, yesterday, today, and tomorrow — that is the dynamic essence of apostolic succession, that basic divine-human continuity in the Church which informs everything else. But we must always remember that the human side of this continuity would never be possible without that marvelous divine preservation which constantly calls the Church out of death into life, setting it free even from itself, for a continued apostolic mission and ministry.

CHAPTER FIVE:

Divine-Human Continuity II

The United Church will be truly evangelical, truly catholic, and truly reformed if, without regarding itself, either an "extension" or a "repetition" of the incarnation, it endeavors to live in continuous response to Christ's one essential, Messianic ministry. For that reason all forms of the Church's ministry must always be submitted to His continuous judgment and mercy. That in turn means that our thankful and hopeful witnessing (or protesting) to Christ's full and free ministry must be coupled with an equally thankful and hopeful witnessing (or protesting) against all who would curtail His sovereign freedom.

"This is a great mystery, and I take it to mean Christ and the church" (Eph. 5:32). These words should always be kept in mind when we try to fathom the dimensional aspects of the divine-human continuity in the life of the Church. For the continuing relationship between Christ and His Church is indeed a great mystery. That predicate can be applied only to the incarnation. The personal union between the awful majesty of God and the humanity of Christ alone is the mystery par excellence. The Church as the Body of the crucified, risen, ascended, and returning Christ is preceded by, and will always remain subordinate to, this unique mystery. Therefore the preeminence of Christ may never be obscured by a deification or mythologization of the Church. Such an obscuring, however, is unavoidable whenever the divine-human continuity in the life of the Church is described as an "extension of the incarnation."

EXTENSION OF THE INCARNATION?

For our present purpose the theologians who define the Christ-Church relationship as an extension of the incarnation may roughly be divided into two groups. To the first belong those who apply this phrase admittedly only as a figure of speech, or uncritically as a useful expression, to indicate that the Church is not merely a voluntary, human society but a fellowship of those who are ruled by the Spirit of Christ and seek to make known, by word and deed, the redemptive significance of the incarnation.[1] We believe, however, that after a critical scrutiny many of these theologians would be willing to drop the phrase "exten-

---

[1] For a comprehensive survey of theologians who use the phrase "extension of the incarnation," see J. Robert Nelson, *The Realm of Redemption*, Epworth Press, 1951, pp. 95-101. See also *The Nature of the Church*, ed. by George W. Richards, Willet Clark and Co., 1945, pp. 28, 42, 51, 61, 74, 96. The content of this book has been incorporated in *The Nature of the Church*, ed. by R. Newton Flew, SCM Press, 1952.

sion of the incarnation," recognizing that it contains a thoroughly unbiblical concept of the Church.

In the second group we find those theologians who regard the Church *literally* an extension of Christ's personality and a prolongation of His atonement. Some of them go so far as to say not only, "Where Christ is, there is the Church," but also, "Where the Church is, there is Christ." It is, of course, rather tempting to conjoin the direct identification of Christ and the Church with a juridically defined doctrine of the apostolic succession. When this occurs, the result is either a pipelined and regimented concept of the Church and its priesthood, as reflected in the doctrine of the Roman Catholic Church, or a "new mystique" as expressed, for example, in the Anglo-Catholic insistence that the Church's "essential" ministry is the so-called "historic episcopate."[2]

Our rejection of the equation "the Church is the extension of the incarnation" is motivated by the following considerations.

(1) Such an equation ultimately destroys the uniqueness and once-for-allness of the hypostatic union of the divine and human natures in Christ, and leads to a mysterious fusion of the divine and human elements in the life of the Church. But we should remember that "It was not the Church that was pre-existent and became incarnate; it was not the Church that was assumed into hypostatic union with the Deity . . . but Jesus Christ alone, the Only-Begotten Son of God."[3]

---

2 See *The Apostolic Ministry: Essays on the History and the Doctrine of Episcopacy,* edited by K. E. Kirk, Hodder and Stoughton, 1946. For a criticism of this view, see T. W. Manson, *The Church's Ministry,* Westminster Press, 1948; T. F. Torrance, *Conflict and Agreement in the Church,* Vol. I., Lutterworth Press, 1959; and *The Catholicity of Protestantism,* edited by R. Newton Flew and Rupert E. Davies, Muhlenberg Press, 1950.

3 T. F. Torrance, *op. cit.,* pp. 15-16.

(2) Ultimately such an equation robs also Christ's atonement from its uniqueness and once-for-allness, either by degrading it into a notion of the "eucharistic sacrifice" as an extension of His priestly sacrifice or by at least binding its effectual communicability to a juridically defined priestly order within the common priesthood of the whole Church. Again we should remember that "It was not the Church that was crucified for our salvation and raised for our justification . . . but Jesus Christ alone, the Only-Begotten Son of God."[4]

(3) A third point to be kept in mind is that the Church is not only a fellowship of *forgiven* sinners but also a fellowship of forgiven *sinners*. When Christ identified Himself with us and shared our human lot, He was tempted in every respect as we are, "yet without sinning" (Heb. 4:15). But our self-identification with Him is never complete, as it is never sinless. Therefore the Church, whose members we are, should not only be humble, as Christ was, but also penitent. If, however, we regard the Church as an extension of His incarnation, it will be much harder for us to resist the temptation not to take our need for continuous forgiveness, repentance, and renewal with utmost seriousness.

(4) Our final observation is that since there is no acceptable theological justification for calling the Church an extension of the incarnation, the line of extension between Christ and His Church is usually sought on the basis of a historical and juridical hypothesis. It is argued that the apostolic authority of the Church is technically transmitted by the rite of the laying on of hands through the unbroken line of the so-called "historic episcopate." But as soon as this happens, the dynamic and spiritual essence of a true apostolic succession is immediately de-

4 *Ibid.*

graded to secondary relevance and it may even be relegated to the background. A horizontal line of descent is assumed between the ministry of the Church and the Jesus of history. At the same time the vertical relationship between the fullness or wholeness of Christ and the wholeness or fullness of the Church is no longer taken seriously, as the historic episcopate is made the "hallmark" of the Church's existence and its veritable guarantor: *ubi episcopus, ibi ecclesia.*[5]

REPETITION OF THE INCARNATION?

But having thus rejected the equation "the Church is the extension of the incarnation," we are still left with the unsolved mystery of the divine-human continuity in the life of the Church. Should this mystery then be described perhaps by another, more appropriate phrase? Should it be called, for example, "a repetition (*Wiederholung*) of the incarnation," as Karl Barth described it in the first volume of his *Church Dogmatics?*[6] We had better be cautious and avoid the usage even of such a phrase, for three reasons.

First of all, in order to avoid certain misunderstandings, its introduction would demand rather elaborate circumscriptions. For example, as Barth himself rightly sensed later, it would need to be stated at once to what extent the existence of the Church *is* a heterogeneous, and to what extent a homogeneous, repetition of the incarnation.

Then, too, the term "repetition" alarmingly reminds us of the Roman Catholic doctrine of the mass which describes the transubstantiation of the elements as a "bloodless repetition" of the sacrifice of Christ on Gol-

[5] Cf. J. A. T. Robinson, "Kingdom, Church and Ministry" in *The Historic Episcopate in the Fullness of the Church,* edited by K. M. Carey, Dacre Press, 1954, p. 19.
[6] *Church Dogmatics,* I, 2, pp. 215-217.

gotha, and also of Bultmann's conception of the existential repetition of Christ's work in the subjective act of faith. Barth himself became aware of all this while writing the fourth volume of his *Church Dogmatics*.[7]

But our main reason for avoiding the usage of the phrase "repetition of the incarnation" is simply this: Christ's "full" and "free" presence is gratuitously *there* in the life of the Church, without a priestly or a subjectivistic repetition of His incarnation, and without rescinding the uniqueness and once-for-allness of it in the fullness of time. It is simply *there* in His continuous self-giving, through Word and sacraments. This divine-human self-giving of Christ alone constitutes and confirms the existence of the Church and enables it continuously *to become the Church,* the ever fresh response to His one essential, Messianic ministry or, in other words, the ever revitalized ministerial Body of the Servant-Lord.

ONE AND MANY

From all that has been said necessarily follows that the divine-human continuity in the life of the Church is thoroughly functional. It can be grasped and ascertained only *in actu:* in the act of the proclamation of the Word, in the act of the administration of the Sacraments, in the act of the exercise of discipline, in the act of pastoral care and counselling, in the act of the Church's upbuilding, and in the act of its evangelism and missionary enterprise. *Many* are, indeed, the forms and versions of the Church's ongoing ministry, but they are all rooted and grounded in their grateful and hopeful response to Christ's *one* Messianic ministry. If anywhere, certainly the Church is the place for us to demonstrate the basic truth element of the

7 *Ibid.,* IV, 1, pp. 767-769.

following apodictic statement: "I respond therefore I am" (*Respondeo, ergo sum*).[8]

The only valid ministry in the life of the Church is the ministry of our Lord.[9] The recipient of this ministry is not simply this or that individual, nor a certain "apostolic college," nor this or that "order" in the Church, but the whole Body. All members of the Body participate in His ministry. In Christ they all share in one common, sacrificing priesthood. They all work together in worshipping God (worship is "service"), in being fellow witnesses for God and in being fellow servants for Him. They all share in the same "inheritance" (*kleros* — share, portion, cf. Acts 26:18, Col. 1:12) by partaking in the ministry of Christ (in this sense they all are "clergymen"); and at the same time they all serve as members of "God's own people" (they are all "laymen"; cf. II Cor. 6:16, I Pet. 2:9). We should never forget that it is this common yet manifold ministry of the whole Church, in response to Christ's one essential, Messianic ministry — and this alone — which shapes it into a worshipping, witnessing, and serving community.

In the life of the New Testament Church this common ministry of the Church was first in a rather fluid state and up till the early part of the second century "there was a good deal of experimenting before detailed patterns of worship and organization began to emerge."[10] Nevertheless, it was felt from the very beginning that to be really the Body of Christ, the Church must be a co-ordinated Body, doing all its work responsibly in the sight of its own

---

[8] Cf. Fritz Heinemann, *Existentialism and the Modern Predicament*, Harper, 1953. In this book a whole chapter is devoted to an analysis of this proposition.

[9] Cf. T. W. Manson, *op. cit.*, pp. 22ff., 33, 107; R. Newton Flew and Rupert E. Davies, *op. cit.*, pp. 104-105.

[10] T. W. Manson, *op. cit.*, p. 71.

Head, which also means in an ontologically well-ordered way (cf. Col. 2:5; I Cor. 14:40, etc.).

"Order" (*taxis,* derived from its verbal form *tasso*) was originally a military term (cf. Matt. 8:9; Luke 7:8). But it has been appropriately introduced in the life of the Church, which on this earth must be a Church Militant since it is permanently involved in godly warfare. Such a Church could certainly not survive, nor lead an exemplary life, without a responsible ordering. And so "order" has become the ontological and historical form for the work of special ministries in the life and ministry of the whole Church.

However, at least four things should always be kept in mind. (1) The divine-human continuity, which is the dynamic essence of apostolic succession and manifests itself in the apostolic mission and ministry of the Church, still remains the function of the whole Body. Nothing less than the entire people of God can be regarded as its organ. From this follows that (2) the ordering of special ministries can never exempt those who are not "ordained," "commissioned," or "consecrated" for these specific functions from continuing to participate in the common ministry of the whole Church. But it also follows that (3) the "apostolicity" of the Church does not depend on any succession within the ordering of special ministries. These ministries may indeed prove to be useful instruments in the life of the Church (otherwise they would not have been "ordered" at all); they may even be regarded as "foci" and "signs" of Christ's presence in the Church; but their "officeholders" do not possess any power, virtue, or authority of their own which they can transmit or confer upon successors. Finally, (4) the "offices" of these special ministries must always be interpreted in a "functional" or "operational" sense, in terms of commission, work, ministry and mission, and not in terms of "position" or "status." The Church as "the earthly-historical form of the existence of Jesus Christ" may work for its fulfillment *through* them but is not at all bound to them.

THE THREE "HISTORIC MINISTRIES"

The number and forms of these special ministries may vary according to the needs of the concrete churches; however, at least three of them have acquired a "historic" character and significance. Their roots can be traced back to the New Testament Church: to the "offices" of deacon, presbyter, and bishop.

(a) *The Deacons.* The first deacons were appointed upon the recommendation of the Church at Jerusalem, by the twelve apostles (Acts 6:1-6). I Timothy 3 gives a definite list of qualifications for the office of deacon but does not describe clearly its functions. From Acts 6:2-3, however, we can infer that the primary duty of deacons was "to serve tables," and to assist the "bishops" or "presbyters" in the administration of the charitable funds of the Church. In the latter half of the second century deacons were no more than the personal assistants of the bishop (see Hippolytus' *Apostolic Tradition* from the first quarter of the third century); and in the Anglican-Episcopal Church of our day they are simply assistant curates to the parish priests under the oversight of the diocesan bishop. There the "diaconate" is a training period during which the deacon is allowed to perform certain restricted functions of the ministry under the guidance of the bishop. However, in certain non-episcopal Protestant churches the deacons are simply the office-bearers of the Church's ministry of compassion, attending to the physical needs of their fellow members.

Whether the "diaconate" is regarded as "the lowest order in the ministry" or simply as one special form of it, we do well to remember three things: (1) It was because of His unique *diakonia* that Jesus was made the Head of the Church and the Lord of the world. (2) As members of His Body, we are all invited (as well as committed) *to serve Him* while serving each other and the world; we are all urged to participate in His *diakonia* and to be incorporated in the universal deaconhood of all believers.[11] (3) The ordering of the "diaconate" as a special form of the Church's ministry certainly does not cancel out the validity of this universal deaconhood; rather it presupposes and helps to fulfill it.

(b) *The Presbyters.* Presbyters are mentioned first in Acts 11:30. There we are told that Barnabas and Saul carried relief to the "elders" of the Christian community at Jerusalem. The presbyters are usually associated with the apostles[12] who, on their journeys abroad, were eager to appoint elders in each new church (Acts 14:23). The twofold function of the presbyters was that of *governing* and *teaching*. From I Timothy 5:17 we gather the impression that not all of them discharged both of these duties; and especially those who were able not only to "rule well" but also to "labor in preaching and teaching" were to be considered "worthy of double honor." Here, then, are to be found the New Testament roots for the office of the "preaching and ruling elders" as they are known today in the Reformed and Presbyterian churches.

The Anglican Church describes presbyters as priests. Some emphasize that the word "priest" is a synonym for "presbyter" or "elder." Others, however, firmly hold that

11 W. A. Visser 't Hooft writes: ". . . the whole Church is called to participate in the comprehensive service. We have as much reason to speak of the general deaconhood of the believers as we have to speak of the general priesthood." (*The Pressure of Our Common Calling*, Doubleday, 1959, p. 48).
12 Acts 15:2, 4, 6, 22, 23; 16:4.

the name "priest" definitely denotes a "sacrificing priest" (a *hiereus* or *sacerdos*), but his act of "offering a sacrifice" should always be interpreted in the context of the uniqueness of Christ's priesthood and of the universal priesthood of the whole Church.[13] The non-episcopal

[13] According to W. Norman Pittenger, the fundamental division between the Anglican and the Protestant views of the ministry is centered not so much in the episcopate itself as in the concept of priesthood. He argues in favor of the usage of the term "sacrificing priesthood" and refers to a statement of the archbishops of Canterbury and York who in 1897, in reply to a bull of Pope Leo XIII, stressed that the eucharist, as celebrated in the Anglican Church, is a "genuine sacrifice" and the priests who offer it are a "sacrificing priesthood" (cf. Pittenger, *The Church, the Ministry, and Reunion*, Seabury Press, 1957, pp. 82-97). But if we compare the statement of the two archbishops concerning the essential elements that make the eucharist a "sacrifice which is offered" with the central prayer in the Order of the Celebration of the Sacrament of the Lord's Supper or Holy Communion as used in the United Presbyterian Church (cf. *The Book of Common Worship*, p. 162), we will be compelled to make the following two, rather striking, observations: (1) The Presbyterian prayer contains references to the same four things which the two archbishops regarded as constitutive of the eucharistic sacrifice, namely, that in it (a) we continue a perpetual memorial of Christ's death and sacrifice, (b) we offer our sacrifice of praise and thanksgiving, (c) we plead His eternal sacrifice, and (d) we offer and present unto God ourselves as living sacrifices. (2) This prayer is offered by the whole congregation and read by an officiating minister even though he has not been ordained in the "order of sacrificing priesthood" by a bishop in the historic episcopate. Yet he is authorized to give vocal expression to this prayer since, together with all the other participants, he has been baptized into the "royal" or "sacrificing priesthood" and individually called and ordered by them (and primarily by God) to serve as His (and their) minister.

The striking resemblance between the definition given by the two archbishops and the text of the Presbyterian prayer clearly indicates that, contrary to Pittenger's opinion, the fundamental division between the Anglican and the Protestant views of the ministry centers not so much in the concept of priesthood as in the *episcopal* ordination. According to the Anglican view, the whole theory of the three orders of the ministry hinges on the validity of such an ordination. This is the "Gordian knot" to be cut by any discussion on church union.

Protestant churches avoid using the term "priest" with reference to any of the special ministries, since it is their desire to stress, on the one hand, the "wholeness" and the "freedom" of Christ's High-priesthood and, on the other hand, the sacrificing priesthood of all believers. Since all Christians are *baptized* into this priesthood, none of them needs to be "ordained" in it. Yet, in the co-ordinated Body of Christ, there is need for the ordained "preaching and/or ruling elders," just as there is for the ordained "deacons."

As in the case of the deacons, here again we may sum up the Christian view in three concise propositions: (1) It was because of His unique *sacrifice* that Jesus was made Head of the Church and Lord of the world. (2) As members of His Body we are all invited (as well as committed) to participate in the common priesthood of all believers. (3) The ordering of the "presbyterate" as another special form of the Church's ministry certainly does not cancel out the validity of this common priesthood; rather it presupposes and helps to fulfill it.

(c) *The Bishops*. The noun *episkopos* (bishop or guardian) occurs only five times in the New Testament, twice in the plural (Phil. 1:1; Acts 20:28), and three times in the singular. In two cases typological descriptions of "the bishop" are given (I Tim. 3:2; Tit. 1:7), and only once is a concrete person singled out and called "bishop." That person is Jesus Christ, "the Shepherd and Guardian [or bishop] of [our] souls" (I Pet. 2:25).

The Septuagint applies the verbal forms *episkeptomai* and *episkopeō*, as well as the noun form *episkopē*, when God's *visitation* (Luther: *Heimsuchung*) is traced in the life of individuals and His people. "Judgment" and "mercy," "punishment" and "salvation" are all connected with this divine visitation (*episkopē*).[14] The care, concern, and friendship of God,[15] but also His wrath and "terrors"[16] are manifested in it. This divine visitation is also pictured as a continuing process, as God's "inquiry" and His never-ceasing "testing" of man.[17]

God's care and concern assumes saving significance, for example, in His gracious visitation of Sarah (Gen. 21:1), or again in the promise given through the dying Joseph that God would visit His people and bring them out of Egypt into the land which he swore to Abraham (Gen. 50:24-25). In the Gospel of Luke, Jesus' birth is hailed as God's gracious visitation with redemptive effect on His people (Luke 1:68, 78), and the Letter to the Hebrews interprets the life and death of Jesus in the same way (2:5ff.). Jesus Himself views His triumphant entry into Jerusalem from the perspective of God's eschatological visitation: He weeps over the inhabitants of the city because they did not know the time of [their] visitation" (Luke 19:44). Rejected by the Jews, God then "visited the Gentiles, to take out of them a people for his name" (Acts 15:14). But even in this gracious act the great "day of visitation" does not yet find its complete fulfillment. That is still in the future (I Pet. 2:12). In the meantime the Church is charged with the exercise of oversight (*episkopē*, I Pet. 5:2), till the day when "the chief Shepherd [shall be] manifested" (5:4), the Shepherd who is called the *episkopos* of souls (2:25).

The next thing to observe is that, according to the New Testament, the Church as a whole and all true followers of Jesus Christ individually are invited and committed to participate in His gracious pastoral care and oversight.

[14] Cf. Exod. 32:34; Isa. 10:3; Hos. 9:7; Jer. 10:15; Zech. 10:3.
[15] Cf. Deut. 11:12; Job 10:12; 29:4.
[16] Cf. Deut. 28:25; Job 6:4.
[17] Cf. Job 7:18; 31:14.

In this respect, we may properly speak not only of the universal deaconhood and priesthood, but also of the universal or corporate "bishophood" *(episkopē)* of all believers.

In His eschatological discourse Jesus stresses that only those who *visited* the sick and the imprisoned will be acknowledged by Him on the last day (Matt. 25:36, 40, 43). And James describes the *visiting* of orphans and widows in their afflictions as a pure and undefiled religious act (James 1:27). The Letter to the Hebrews, by using the verb *episkopein,* in the sense of "looking diligently," "seeing to," or "caring for something," makes it the responsibility of the whole congregation to protect and promote the salvation, peace, and moral integrity of each individual member (12:15-16). Hermann W. Beyer is correct in observing: "It is significant . . . that a task which later on became the specific obligation of one man, namely the leader of the congregation, is here presented as the concern of the whole Church. The entire community as such is here understood as bearer of an office and ministry which is episcopal in its very nature."[18]

Turning now to the plural use of the noun *episkopos,* we have to note first of all that the apostles and prophets are never called *episkopoi.* On the other hand, the name "bishops" always occurs as a synonym for the name "elders."[19] In this respect the most remarkable passage is Paul's admonishment to the Ephesian *elders:* "Take heed to yourselves and to all the flock, in which the Holy Spirit has made you guardians [*episkopous*], to feed the church of the Lord, which he obtained with his own blood" (Acts 20:28). This verse, together with the other already noted biblical references, clearly indicates also that the work of

[18] Cf. Hermann Wolfgang Beyer's article in Kittel's *Theologisches Wörterbuch,* II, 600.
[19] Cf. Phil 1:1; Acts 20:17; I Tim. 3:1-7; 5:17-19; Tit. 1:5-9.

exercising the oversight *(episkopē)* was primarily a spiritual-pastoral and only secondarily a governmental task. Yet the two could not be separated one from the other.

The name *presbyteroi* was used in Christian congregations of Jewish origin, while the word *episkopoi* was used primarily in congregations of Greek origin. But in every instance both names expressed nothing else but the unpretentious participation of these office-bearers in the total ministry of Jesus Christ without their claiming for themselves any power. Of a monarchical episcopate we find not even the slightest traces in the New Testament. Yet it is psychologically quite understandable that the admonition to give "double honor" to outstanding elders (I Tim. 5:17) may have opened the door for the "bishop-in-presbyterate" or the "corporate episcopate" in which one outstanding elder was called "bishop" and did the work of presiding, leading, and governing. Nevertheless, he still remained in close association with the other elders.

We sum up the basic Christian view in regard to the third historic ministry, called the episcopate, in the following three propositions. (1) It is because of the unique visitation *(episkopē)* of a seeking God in Jesus Christ that we place our faith in Him as the Head of the Church and the Lord of the world. (2) As members of His Body, we are all invited (as well as committed) to participate in His constant care, concern, and visitation *(episkopē)*, and thus we are all incorporated in the general or corporate "bishophood"[20] *(episkopē)* of all believers. (3) The ordering of the "episcopate" as a third, special form of the Church's ministry certainly does not cancel out the

[20] I am aware of the fact that the word "bishophood" is not an accepted English term. However, since we speak of "priesthood," and as footnote 11 indicates of "deaconhood," why could we not adopt the word "bishophood"? I feel that here it is more appropriate to speak of the "bishophood" than of the "bishopric" or "episcopate" of all believers.

validity of this corporate "bishophood" *(episkopē)*; rather it presupposes and helps to fulfill it.

"HAVE MERCY UPON US!"

We conclude with one more comment on the three historic ministries of the Church, or rather on all the possible forms of the ministry which have emerged in the past, or may emerge in the future, life of the Church.

T. W. Manson, at the end of his excellent discourse on what he calls "the settled ministry," makes the observation that in the *Apostolic Tradition* of Hyppolytus the prayer for the consecration of a bishop is a prayer of invocation, an *epiklesis*. The same holds true in the case of the ordination of a presbyter and of a deacon, and also in the case of the initiation of church members. He interprets all this to mean that, "while each of these has his own function in the common life of the Body of Christ, and while there are ordered relations among them of coordination or subordination, they are all alike in this, that all depend completely on the one essential ministry, that of Christ Himself in His Church."[21]

This complete dependence on His ministry is our great equalizer. This comes to expression very meaningfully in the *Kyrie,* as we all pray together, "Lord, have mercy upon *us*" — not only upon the baptized members but also upon the ordained ministers. For whether we are bishops, presbyters, deacons, or any other office-bearers in the Church, we, too, bear the signs of an "ambiguous existence," just as much as all the other members of the Church do. We, too, are at once sinners and sanctified. We, too, fall continuously under God's judgment and are in dire need of His mercy.

That one short pronoun in the *Kyrie,* the very last

21 *Op. cit.,* pp. 81-82.

word "us," repeated by minister and congregation alike, gathers up and includes all who are members of Christ's Body, His holy catholic Church. In it the universal deaconhood, the common priesthood, and the corporate bishophood of all believers as well as the various ministries of the ordained office-bearers (deacons, presbyters, and bishops alike), all converge into one continuously revitalized ministry as they are continuously submitted to His judgment and to His mercy.

As long as we are ready to pray the *Kyrie* together, sincerely and without any mental reservation, we shall certainly be strengthened by His Spirit to witness thankfully and hopefully *to* Christ's full and free presence and ministry in the Church, and to witness courageously *against* all who would curtail His sovereign freedom. And we shall also find ourselves "walking," "working," "serving," and "growing" *together* in the Church's continuously ongoing movement of apostolic succession.

CHAPTER SIX:

Divine-Human Continuity III

The United Church will be truly evangelical, truly catholic, and truly reformed if, without binding Christ's one essential Messianic ministry to any one of the "historic ministries" of the Church, it endeavors to make the best possible use of each, being fully aware of the fact that the Holy Spirit can and may exercise His sovereign freedom in creating and using new forms for the Church's continuing ministry. For that reason all teachings concerning an authorized ministry and hence also all the diverging interpretations of the so-called "historic episcopate" must be submitted to His continuous judgment and mercy. That in turn means that in a United Church opportunity must be given for a twofold witnessing. On the one hand there must be a thankful witnessing (or protesting) to the fact that in the past Christ has blessed both the episcopal and the non-episcopal ministries coupled with a hopeful expectancy that His blessing will become even more manifest in our reordered and reconstituted ministries. On the other hand, the right will have to be assured to all who want to do so to witness (or protest) against any endeavor that would make the episcopal succession an exclusive channel for the grace of God and a condition for its ministration in the Church, thus curtailing the freedom of Christ's continuous ministry.

The first two of these introductory theses contain the conclusions of the two preceding chapters. Now these conclusions will have to be applied to the problems connected with the reconstitution of a unified ministry, and especially to the problems raised by the "historic episcopate."

THE GORDIAN KNOT

Eugene C. Blake in his sermon referred to these problems as "the Gordian knot of hundreds of years of controversy" which needs to be cut "by establishing in the United Church a historic ministry recognized by all without doubt or scruple." This was obviously an allusion to Alexander the Great who, finding himself unable to unravel the Gordian knot, the ends of which were secretly twisted around and folded up within it, simply cut it apart with his sword.

Alexander's act was indeed a radical one. It certainly untied the knot but at the same time produced a lot of "loose ends." The great question our reunion negotiations encounter is this: Can we be as radical as Alexander in cutting the Gordian knot of controversies concerning the "historic episcopate" without at the same time letting loose a multitude of new problems and ending up with new controversies and new divisions?

There is one sound answer to this question: Yes, we can, provided that we let the Word of God and the Holy Spirit do the "cutting." By taking "the sword of the Spirit, which is the word of God" (Eph. 6:17), and letting it pierce as far as the place where our ecclesiastical traditions divide, and by letting it sift the purposes and thoughts of our hearts, we certainly shall be able to find a basis for a unified and authorized ministry.

But let us not deceive ourselves, for such a "cutting" does not mean a push-button short cut. It will demand from our uniting churches much penitence for their divisiveness, much gratitude for the presence of Christ in the past both in the episcopal and the non-episcopal ministries, much hope and expectancy that His continuous self-giving will become even more manifest in our re-ordered and reconstituted ministries, much love and understanding toward one another even if we happen to differ in our interpretations and, above all, much dependence on, and obedience to, the Holy Spirit and the Holy Scriptures as the norm of all Christian teaching and practice.

ENDEAVORS TO DO THE "CUTTING"

In the last two decades various attempts have been made to do this "cutting." We shall mention here only five of them and describe briefly their ecumenical relevance.

(a) *The Church of South India.* This Church came into being in 1947.[1] Its constitution provides for the

---

[1] There is a rather extensive literature on the Church of South India. We mention here only a few titles: A. Dammers, *Great Venture: The Church of South India in Action*, London, Highway Press, 1958; Stephen Neil, "A Dangerous Experiment: The Church of South India" in *Christian Partnership*, 1952; J. E. Lesslie Newbigin, *That All May Be One: A South India Diary, The Story of An Experiment*

preservation of the episcopal succession. At the same time it regards all the existing ministers, whether episcopally ordained or not, as fully authorized ministers of the Church. For a period of thirty years ministers not episcopally ordained can be received into this church's ministry, and only at the end of that period will the final decision be made whether the Church of South India will ultimately require episcopal ordination as the condition for the recognition of other ministers, or whether the present condition will be continued indefinitely.

Fifteen years have elapsed and the Church of South India is still in an experimental stage. The radical cutting of the Gordian knot has been postponed in the life of this church but there is hope that before the end of the thirty-year period events both inside and outside of it will prepare the way to make the cutting easy and smooth. The Church of South India is certainly an exciting experiment in Christian partnership which may slowly but surely pave the way to organic unity.

(b) *The North India-Pakistan Plan.* For many years a negotiating committee for church union has been at work also in North India and Pakistan. It produced a *Plan of Church Union*[2] which tries to do the cutting of the Gordian knot of controversies by finding a way to put all the ministers on a truly equal basis from the very beginning.

---

in Christian Unity, New York, Association Press, 1952; *The Reunion of the Church: A Defense of the South India Scheme,* rev. edition, London, SCM Press, 1960.

2 *Plan of Church Union in North India and Pakistan,* third, revised edition, 1957. This work was published for the Negotiating Committee by the Christian Literature Society and printed at the Diocesan Press, Madras, 1957. See also Stephen F. Bayne, Jr., *Ceylon, North India, Pakistan: A Study in Ecumenical Decision,* S.P.C.K., 1960; Lewis S. Mudge, "The Plan of Union in North India and Pakistan: A Theological Analysis," *Bulletin of the Department of Theology,* World Alliance of Reformed Churches, Summer, 1962, Vol. 3, No. 1.

This plan pronounces the episcopate as both "constitutional" and "historic," and defines the "historic episcopate" as "the episcopate which is in historic continuity with that of the early Church." It also hastens to declare that "the Church is not committed thereby to any one particular theological interpretation of episcopacy, nor does it demand the acceptance of such an interpretation from its ministers and members."

The plan then proposes a unique ceremony for the unification of ministers. One representative minister from each of the seven uniting churches will lay hands on three ministers, who have been chosen beforehand, and one of whom is a bishop, and will commission them to the ministry of presbyters (and bishop) of the Church of God within the Church of North India and Pakistan. Then the three newly commissioned ministers in turn will lay hands on the seven representative ministers. In this way first the new Church *with its ministry* (i.e., the presbyterate, which includes one bishop) comes into being, and the declaration and confirmation of the Bishops Designate, as well as the consecration of the new bishops only, follow this "representative act of unification of the ministry." It is also stressed that "the use of this rite does not imply a denial of the ordination previously received by those now seeking to become presbyters of the Church of North India and Pakistan; it is not reordination, nor is it presumed to bestow again the grace, gifts, character or authority that have already been bestowed upon them."

The approval of this plan by all the churches involved is still uncertain. The principles laid down in it can not be spelled out here in all their details. But those mentioned here will certainly have a wholesome effect upon all future union negotiations.

(c) *Anglican-Presbyterian Conversations.* In the 1950's conversations were held between representatives of the

Episcopal and Presbyterian churches in Great Britain. The results of these conversations were published in 1957 under the title *Relations Between Anglican and Presbyterian Churches*.[3]

This report does not envisage a church union but only full intercommunion, "involving fully authorized interchange of communications and mutual recognition of ministries." The latter would be made possible by "the acceptance of the 'historic episcopate' by the Presbyterian churches . . . and the acceptance of a greater measure of 'corporate episcopacy' by the Anglican churches." It is argued that in the Church of Scotland the presbytery is practically a "corporate episcopate" while in the Church of England the functions of the "historic episcopate" converge in a single person. An assimilation of these two types of episcopate would mean that the Presbyterians would have to set apart a moderator as a permanent "bishop in presbytery," and the Episcopalians would have to integrate the bishop more closely with the presbyterate and the laity in his synod so that he could become a "bishop in synod." The report proposes a mutual commissioning of authority between the Episcopalian bishops and the Presbyterian presbyteries. Such a commissioning would not mean reordination of ministers or reconsecration of bishops but a mutual act of prayer and laying on of hands by which all would enter the responsible ministerial authority of the other as well as of their own church.

The new bishops in the Presbyterian churches would be chosen by each presbytery from their own membership

[3] Edinburgh, St. Andrew Press; London, S.P.C.K., 1957. See also T. F. Torrance, *Conflict and Agreement in the Church*, Lutterworth Press, 1959, I, 104-105; Arthur C. Cochrane, "Common Presuppositions of the Report on Relations Between Anglican and Presbyterian Churches," *McCormick Quarterly*, Vol. XV, March 1962, No. 3.

or otherwise, and would initially be consecrated by the laying on of hands by bishops from one or more of the Episcopal churches and by appointed representatives of the presbytery. In the Episcopalian churches "lay persons would be solemnly 'set apart' for some measure of pastoral responsibility towards their fellow Christians," and at all levels of the government of the church they would be "integrated" with the bishops and presbyters to discharge the corporate responsibility of the whole Church.

The great merits of this report are: (a) Its definition of the Church as the Body of Christ that participates in His threefold ministry as Prophet, Priest and King. (b) Its emphasis that every ministry in the Church is a ministry exercised within the corporate priesthood of all believers. (c) Its emphasis on the specific ministry of Word and sacrament as well as of the *episcopē* or oversight in the Church, stressing that all these are valid only in the context of the corporate responsibility of the *whole* Church.

(d) *Towards Unity in Australia.* The ideas of "bishop in presbytery" and "corporate episcopate" have been happily adopted and utilized by a Joint Commission on Church Union representing the Congregational, Methodist and Presbyterian churches in Australia.[4] Though none of these churches belongs to the Episcopalian tradition, yet in their proposed constitution for the uniting Church in Australia they definitely plan for a new form of ministry, calling it "the bishop-in-presbytery." They prefer the less ambiguous word "presbyter" rather than the more general term "minister." Their presbyters would

---

4 See *The Church: Its Nature, Function and Orderings* (Being the Second Report of the Joint Commission on Church Union Together with the Proposed Basis of Union for The Congregational Churches of Australia, The Methodist Church of Australasia, and The Presbyterian Church of Australia), The Aldersgate Press, Melbourne, 1963.

be ordained at a laying-on-of-hands ceremony by a "bishop-in-presbytery" and at least three other presbyters. Some of their presbyters could then be appointed bishops whose personal *episcopē,* however, should be exercised only within the corporate *episcopē* of the presbyters, and they would remain answerable to the church councils.

The members of the Australian Joint Commission, at least the majority of them, prudently discerned that by introducing the office of "bishop-in-presbytery" the new Church would have in its constitution "the reformed episcopacy" and would be better prepared for a concordat with the Church of South India which is an episcopally ordered Church. They also hoped that in this way they would hasten unity with the Church of England in Australia, which is by far the largest church on that continent.

The Australian step should certainly be regarded as another endeavor to cut the Gordian knot of centuries-old controversies as smoothly as possible and to pave the way for the gradual establishment of a unified ministry.

(e) *Anglican-Methodist Conversations.* Last, but not least, we refer to the conversations between the Church of England and the Methodist Church. These conversations have finally resulted in a printed report which Thomas F. Torrance called "the most crucial report on inter-church relations yet published."

The basic proposals in this report are that the Church of England and the Methodist Church should move toward union in two steps. The first would be a period of prayer and study that would lead to the formal acceptance of the proposals for the achievement of full communion between the two churches. Provided that these necessary preliminaries are settled, a comprehensive act of reconciliation involving services throughout the two churches could then take place. The service of reconciliation would include a formal reception of the members

111

and ministers of one church by accredited representatives of the other, authorizing each member to communicate and each bishop, priest, and minister to officiate in either church.

The second step would follow only after many years of continuing partnership and full communion between the two churches and would be concluded by the final achievement of organic union.

The unification of the ministries would take place in the first stage. Since the "historic episcopate" is "an inalienable element in the Anglican inheritance," the Methodists are ready to assimilate it. At the same time, however, "they ask for assurance that . . . no interpretation making episcopal ordination essential to the being of the Church and episcopal succession an exclusive channel of the grace of God" would be declared "a condition of the ministration of the grace of God in the Church." Provided that the same freedom of integration would be granted to the Methodists which "the Anglicans now enjoy in respect to the historic episcopate," the service of reconciliation could be followed very soon by the consecration of bishops elected by the Methodist Conference for the Methodist Church. "Thereafter it would be the rule in the Methodist Church that all ordination of ministers would be by bishops, assisted by other ministers."[5]

One may find certain theologically questionable verbs, phrases, and statements in this report. For example, the episcopate certainly does not "secure" the apostolic mission and authority within the Church (as stated in the report, p. 24). It can only "attest to" or "guard" them. Again, one must wonder whether the phrase "the strictest

[5] *Conversations Between The Church of England and The Methodist Church: A Report to the Archbishops of Canterbury and York and the Conference of the Methodist Church,* Church Information Carey, Dacre Press, 1954, pp. 105-127.

invariability of episcopal ordination" (p. 48) can be regarded as compatible with the doctrine of the freedom of Christ and the Holy Spirit. Then, too, the ambiguous use of the word "catholic" should have been avoided in such a historic document. The Methodists, too, are "catholics" ("evangelical" or "protesting catholics," to be sure), and only an equivocal use of the word "catholic" can account for such a statement as follows: "Union between the Methodists and the Church of England means that Methodists will live not only with evangelicals but with catholics" (p. 49). As it now reads in the Service of Reconciliation (pp. 42, 46), the spirit of true catholicity is certainly better expressed in the words of the presiding minister of the Methodist Church than in the words of the bishop of the Anglican Church. For while the former says to the representative members of the Church of England: "In the name of God . . . we . . . welcome you . . . into fellowship with us in *Christ's Church*" (which necessarily can mean only the one holy catholic Church), the bishop of the Church of England "receives" the members of the Methodist Church "into the fellowship of *the Church of England*" (which, however catholic it may be, can certainly not be regarded identical with the one holy catholic Church).

These critical comments notwithstanding, we can only rejoice in the fact that the Anglican-Methodist conversations on church union have produced such a promising document. The union movements throughout the whole world seem to tend toward a happy combination of Episcopal, Presbyterian and Congregational church polities. Thus, for example, John Marsh, himself a leading Congregationalist in England, recently acknowledged the necessity of introducing "true episcopacy" in the forthcoming United Church. In a call made to the Congregational Union of England and Wales, he stated:

... there is no possible hope of attaining any comprehensive church unity . . . unless the united body be an episcopal church. Our duty is not to oppose the word episcopacy, however much it may have been misused in the past, but to share with our fellow Christians in the search, which is by no means a blind or unhopeful one, for its true meaning, and for the full and rich reality of a true episcopacy to be embodied in a united church. I do not believe this is impossible or impracticable, but possible and necessary . . . .[6]

In the preceding chapter the New Testament bases for a true episcopacy have already been explored. Our remaining task is to give a critical summary of the various interpretations of the "historic episcopate" as they exist side by side in the Anglican-Episcopal churches.

THREE DIVERGING VIEWS

The first view,[7] usually called the "high-Anglican" or the "Anglo-Catholic" view, makes the "historic episcopate" a prerequisite for the very being (*esse*) of the Church. Where there is no bishop consecrated in the "historic episcopate" (i.e., within the line of "apostolic succession") there can be no Church. The bishop is *the only means* by which Christ's commission is given anew to each new minister of His Church. Without episcopal ordination there can be no valid ministry and hence no priesthood to celebrate the eucharist. The bishop is *the guarantee* and *the principal organ* of the Church's continuity in apostolic teaching and administration and of its unity. Only a church which possesses the "historic episcopate" is within the covenant. All other churches are outside of the Body

[6] See *The British Weekly*, May 16, 1963, Vol. CXLVII, No. 3982.
[7] See, for example, K. E. Kirk, *The Apostolic Ministry*, Hodder and Stoughton, 1946.

and belong only to the "soul of the Church." Their ministries are non-episcopal, and for that reason they can receive and transmit only the uncovenanted grace of God.

The second view differs from the first mainly in not regarding the "historic episcopate" as essential to the Church.[8] At the same time it stresses that it is a necessary mark of its fullness. Without the "historic episcopate" the Church cannot express the plenitude of its being (its *plene esse*) as the one Body of Christ.

Churches which do not possess the "historic episcopacy" lack something of the fullness of Christ. That "something" is the apostolic ministry which has for its channel the "apostolic succession" as the outside sign and instrument of the Church's unity. Only bishops who stand in this succession, i.e., in a succession of episcopal consecration and ordination, are the full embodiment of the gospel in church order, the effectual symbol of apostolic continuity and unity, and of the relation of Christ to His Church. Thus episcopacy is not merely a particular form of church organization. It must be integrated theologically as the office of oversight, the seat of authority, and the fount of ministry. It serves as a living link between the Church of today and of yesterday. It protects the deposits of faith and guards the wholeness of the apostolic message. In administering the sacraments of confirmation, ordination and consecration, the bishop helps the Church to realize its true nature and to show forth the stature of the fullness of Christ. Any consultation on church union will have to come to terms with the "historic episcopate," since without it the Church's ministry would remain defective, and the Church itself could not be fully one, catholic, or apostolic.

[8] See H. W. Montefiore, "The Historic Episcopate," in *The Historic Episcopate in the Fulness of the Church,* edited by Kenneth M. Carey, Dacre Press, 1954, pp. 105-127.

The third view, mostly the view of the so-called "Anglican Evangelicals," regards the episcopacy as a relevant contributing factor to the *bene esse* (well-being) of the Church.[9] It believes that the "historic episcopate" constitutes an important expression of the continuity of the Church in time, and of the unity of its fellowship across space. Thus it is a "valuable" and "good" arrangement. However, this view does not tie the apostolic ministry to the historic "apostolic succession," nor does it limit the latter to episcopal ordination and consecration. It finds the focus of apostolicity in the identity of the gospel (which "neither grows nor develops") and in the ever fresh and new fidelity of the whole Church as well as of the officeholders to the original testimony of the apostles. It does entertain a high view of the necessity of order and of rightful ordination into the ministry but believes that every minister of the non-episcopal communions, if duly called and commissioned to act as such, participates in the one prophetic, priestly, and kingly ministry of Christ no less than do his Anglican brethren. Finally, it stresses that in the coming great Church all the existing orders heretofore used and sanctioned by our Lord will find their reintegration and fulfillment.

We shall be brief in our appraisal of these views. The first view is unacceptable to all who regard the Kingdom of God in Christ as the *only* reason for the Church's existence. Basing the *esse* of the Church on a linear succession of bishops means essentially replacing Christ rather than representing Him, and making the bishop the guarantee of the Church's continuity and unity is to introduce a false sense of security in its life. The covenanting act of God with His people is certainly not "cabin'd, cribb'd,

9 See, for example, F. J. Taylor, *The Church of God,* London, 1946.

116

and confined" to churches which possess the "historic episcopate."

The second view, because it proceeds from the New Testament concept of the "fullness of Christ," proves to be much more biblical than the first. However, it soon gets sidetracked from the original biblical position which describes the relationship between Christ's fullness and that of the Church as thoroughly eschatological and as constantly exposed to Christ's judgment and mercy. For that reason, none of the so-called orders in themselves, not even the "historic episcopate," but the gospel ministry alone (and that again only as the total ministry of the *whole* Church), can make the "fullness" and "freedom" of Christ manifest in the life of the Church.

Both views agree that the bishop is the fount of ministry and the seat of authority, but neither of them can refer to any adequate biblical evidence, nor mobilize any acceptable theological reasons for proving their position. In the New Testament Christ alone (and not the episcopacy) "is the Fount of all, of the Church, the Ministry, the Fellowship."[10] Episcopacy may well express this fellowship but it certainly does not determine it. It may well be an outward symbol of the inward unity and continuity of the Church, but it certainly is not an *effectual* symbol of it.[11] If it were, this would make it another sacrament. The fact that in the Anglican-Episcopal Church confirmation, ordination, and consecration are definitely episcopal acts, associated with, and limited to, the sole jurisdiction of the bishops, certainly betrays a strong leaning in that direction. And with regard to unification of the ministries of episcopal and non-episcopal

[10] John Line, *The Doctrine of the Christian Ministry,* Lutterworth Press, 1959, p. 109.

[11] Cf. T. F. Torrance, *Royal Priesthood,* Oliver and Boyd, 1955, p. 107.

churches, this is indeed the one great obstacle to be overcome.

Yet we are optimistic. Our hopefulness is strengthened by two encouraging facts. The first is that in the Anglican-Episcopal churches there is no explicit and binding doctrine of the episcopacy. This makes it possible for the various adherents of these three views to live and work together in the same Church. The second encouraging fact is the growing number of Anglican Evangelicals whose view can be easily harmonized with the concept of "corporate episcopate" or "bishop-in-presbyterate" as practiced in principle in certain Protestant churches. (See, for example, the "parish episcopate" in the Reformed Church of France, and the presbyterial bishops or superintendents in the Reformed Church of Hungary.) Any discussion on church union will have to move along the line of mutually integrating "historic episcopate" and the "corporate episcopate" or "bishop-in-presbyterate" as exemplified or proposed by certain non-episcopal churches. Such an integration could be hastened if both sides heeded the objective, scholarly observation of J. B. Lightfoot, the late bishop of Durham:

> . . . the episcopate was formed not out of the apostolic order by localisation but out of the presbyteral by elevation: and the title, which originally was common to all, came at length to be appropriated to the chief among them.[12]

Theses for Unification

The following ten theses are presented as humble suggestions or guide lines in furthering the cause of the reunification of Christian ministries. By no means should

[12] J. B. Lightfoot, *Saint Paul's Epistle to the Philippians,* Macmillan, 1903, p. 196.

they be regarded as final or apodictic. They represent a certain stage in the author's thinking and are open for further revisions and amendments. Some of the words and phrases used in these theses were freely borrowed from the various union proposals, plans, and reports. After all, if anywhere, it is here that the concert of Christian minds throughout the whole world should become clearly manifest. These theses also serve as a summary of the last three chapters on divine-human continuity in the life of Christ's Church.

(1) The Church as the Body of Christ is theandric in its nature, that is, it is rooted and grounded in the mystery of divine-human continuity.

(2) The divine element of this continuity is the ever full and ever free presence or self-giving of the crucified and risen Lord. His one essential, Messianic ministry manifests itself in His unique servanthood (*diakonia*), priesthood (*hierosunē*), and bishophood (*episcopē*). As our ever available Servant (*diakonos*), as our only High Priest (*archiereus*), and as *the* Bishop (*episkopos*) of our souls, Jesus Christ is the sole Head (*kephalē*) of the Church and the sole Lord (*kurios*) of the world.

(3) The human element of this continuity is similarly functional and ministerial. The Church lives in utter dependence on Christ's full and free self-giving, yet in a relation of personal interdependence with Him. The Church's response is always a responsible one, namely, its offering of itself to Christ and its offering of Christ to the world. However, this response could never be possible without that marvelous divine preservation which constantly calls the Church out of death into life, setting it free even from itself, for a continued apostolic mission and ministry.

(4) This divine-human continuity in the life of the Church informs everything else. It is the continuing move-

ment of apostolic succession, not limited only to office-holders; it is a thankful and a hopeful obedience of the Church to the "whole" Christ and the "free" Christ; a continuous dying *with* Him and living *in* Him; the growth of the total Body from "fullness" to "fullness" until its members attain to the measure of the stature of the fullness of Him who fills all in all.

(5) This divine-human continuity comes to expression in the ministry of the whole Church. For the Church not only has a ministry; it *is* through and through ministry — the actual and factual communication of the Word through witness and service, sealed by the two sacraments, namely, Baptism, which is the sacrament of our once-for-all incorporation into Christ, and the Lord's Supper (or eucharist), which is the sacrament of our continued renewal in this incorporation. In and through the proclamation of the Word and the administration of the sacraments the members of the Church participate in the unique servanthood, priesthood and bishophood of Jesus Christ. And it is in and through this participation that they are joined together in the one Body.

(6) God's will demands that in the life of the Church Militant the work of the ministry should transpire specifically through the ordering of the Church. For that reason, Christ's "charismatic" ministry is offered to the Church in a variety of gifts, which in turn opens up ever new possibilities for service to Him. In the midst of the Church's continuous ministry there are especially three orders or offices which have endured throughout the centuries, namely, that of deacon, that of the presbyter (or priest), and that of the bishop. They all point beyond themselves as they help to bring to fulfillment the universal deaconhood, the common priesthood, and the corporate bishophood of all believers. God's work, however, is never bound to any of them, since He reserves His freedom with re-

gard to all His orderings to make any altered situation in the life of His Church amendable to His unchanging ends.

(7) Since any order or office in the evangelical, catholic, and reformed Church must be interpreted in terms of "subministration," i.e., as a dependent, derivative, functional ministry, in responsible response to Christ's one essential and constitutive ministry, this also applies to the office of bishop. In the context of the universal deaconhood of all believers, he is the servant of all the servants of God (*servus servorum Dei*). In the context of the common priesthood of all believers, he is the chief *ordinator* and the pastor of pastors (*pastor pastorum*). And in the context of the corporate bishophood of all believers, he is the chief *visitator*, overseer, and the leader of the practical administration in the diocese (presbytery), and is consecrated to the office of bishop by one or more bishops in co-operation with delegated presbyters of the diocese (presbytery). His consecration does not bestow upon him any new power or gift (*charisma*) which he did not exercise or possess before as a member of the ordained ministry. He discharges the ministry of his office as first among equals (*primus inter pares*), as a bishop in the presbyterate, and as one who is responsible primarily to Christ (the Servant Lord, the High Priest, and the Bishop of all souls), and secondarily to the presbytery (corporate episcopate). By no means is he to be regarded or even adored as the vicegerent of Christ and as the fount of a hierarchically structured ministry.

(8) Since the Anglican-Episcopal Church has shown to the whole ecclesiastical world that it is possible to have bishops in the historic succession without insisting upon any explicit and binding doctrine regarding it, a re-united Church must do the same thing. Without declaring any particular doctrine of the episcopacy, it must allow its members, deacons, presbyters and bishops to hold freely

any of the already existing three views in regard to the episcopate. (The office of the bishops belongs (a) to the very being [*esse*], (b) to the fullness [*plene esse*], or (c) to the well-being [*bene esse*] of the Church). Some may even work out a fourth and a fifth view or theory, should they find it necessary to do so. What must be binding on all is simply this: No one member, deacon, presbyter, or bishop in the reunited Church must hold any view in regard to the ordering of the ministry (specifically, in regard to the episcopacy) that is an encroachment on the full and free lordship of Christ, i.e., on His unique servanthood, priesthood or bishophood. On the contrary, their thankful and hopeful witnessing *to* Christ's free and full lordship, presence, and ministry must always be coupled with an equally thankful and hopeful witnessing *against* all who would curtail His sovereign freedom.

(9) To establish a historic ministry recognized by all, such a ministry must be initiated by the United Church in a solemn, representative act of unification or reconciliation. Such an act must be neither ordination nor re-ordination but a third rite, pointing beyond both, as a sign of the renewal of the whole Church. In this act of unification the uniting churches must mutually acknowledge each other's ministries as blessed and used by the Holy Spirit and as ministries of Christ in His Word and sacraments. They must further acknowledge that hitherto all of their ministries have been limited in scope and authority, not having the seal of the whole Church. Therefore, without adopting any particular theory of historic succession, by the mutual laying on of hands, in a solemn act of humility and re-dedication with prayer, the consecration of the bishops of the United Church must take place with participation of bishops and presbyters both in the "historic succession" and outside of it from all of the uniting churches. This first representative act of uni-

fication must then be followed by similar services of unification in the newly formed dioceses (presbyteries), at which all the formerly consecrated bishops and ordained presbyters seek together from God and for themselves whatever of the fullness of Christ's grace, commission, and authority each may need for the exercise of his new and larger ministry.

In this act of unification any difference that existed between ministers not episcopally ordained and those already so ordained is then to be regarded as transcended so that the United Church can receive, at its inception, a ministry fully and without exception accredited in the eyes of all its members and, as far as possible, in the eyes of the Church throughout the world.

It is hoped that, by the grace of God, these solemn services of unification or reconciliation will be followed by the continuous process of growing into ever deeper unity in which all at every place will be constantly mobilized by the Spirit in all the dimensions of their evangelical, catholic, and reformed faith. Then they will become more and more joint-partakers in the gospel, i.e., partners in obedience to Christ's full self-giving, partners in gratitude for His free presence with the Church in the past and partners in hope anchored in this presence with regard to the future, partners in outgoing love toward all for whom He died, and partners in a continuously ongoing repentance, renewal, and reform in the sight of the Lord who will certainly reward such a partnership with ultimate unity.

(10) Last but not least, such an evangelical, catholic, and reformed Church must not regard its own unity and continuity as ends in themselves but make them subservient to the Kingdom of God in Christ through its never-ceasing, ever-increasing missionary enterprise in and for the world. It must have one ultimate concern, namely,

to unite all things in Christ. To that end it must be constantly, fully, and sincerely committed to Him whose "fullness" is ultimate and whose "faithfulness" is the perfection of His "freedom."

The delineation of this ultimate concern and these ever new commitments in the life of a Church truly evangelical, truly catholic, and truly reformed will engage our attention in the final two chapters of this book.

CHAPTER SEVEN:

The Church's Ultimate Concern

The ultimate concern of a truly evangelical, truly catholic, and truly reformed Church can be nothing less than the service of God's glory through the restoration of the whole world. For that reason, the breadth *of our faith will have to be determined by the* finality *of Christ as it demands from us a compassionate* love *to all men. And as the breadth of our faith meets with its height and its length, the movement of apostolic succession is constantly translated into the apostolic mission and ministry of the Church. That in turn means that the Church, as the ministerial and missionary Body of Christ, must serve both as a* beachhead *and as a* bridge. *And as we endeavor to speak and to do the truth in the spirit of Christ's* agapē-love, *our witnessing (or protesting) attitude will necessarily manifest itself in a twofold ministry: the ministry of* rebuke *and that of* reconciliation.

Our first two basic concepts were control and continuity. The third is *concern*. What is the Church's ultimate concern? To answer this question, the Church must be viewed from the perspective of a dynamic intertexture.

A Dynamic Intertexture

The components of this intertexture can be described only in terms of basic relationships. The first is the Christ-world relationship: the crucified and risen Lord is the Head over all things (Eph. 1:22). The second is the Christ-Church relationship: the Lord of the world is also the Head of the Church (Eph. 4:15; etc.). The third is the Christ-Kingdom relationship: with the coming of Christ the Kingdom of God has become a present reality (Matt. 3:2), though its ultimate fulfillment is still in the future (Rev. 11:15). The fourth is the Church-world relationship: the Church is *in* the world, *for* the world, yet not *of* the world (John 17:14, 23). Finally, the Church-Kingdom relationship: since God's ultimate purpose in Christ is to establish His Kingdom on the earth, the Church's ultimate concern can only be an unconditional response to this divine purpose. The Church is here to represent Christ to the world and to turn the whole earth into a "theatre of God's glory" (Calvin). The Church's concern is certainly not its own creation. It only re-echoes the mandate given by Christ. And it is final, ultimate, because its Mandator is ultimate. And so the basic fact on which the whole concern of the entire Church hinges is the *finality* of Christ.

The Finality of Christ

The "finality" of Christ means, first of all, that in Him, that is, in His birth, life, death, resurrection, and ascension, God the Father has brought to fulfillment the redemption of the whole world.

Secondly, it means that whatever God has done in Jesus Christ He will not repeat. The events known as the incarnation, the crucifixion, the resurrection, and the ascension were unique, once-for-all events. They cannot be repeated; nor can they be continued or extended.

Thirdly, the finality of Christ means that He is the exclusive Lord of the whole world. His Lordship is an absolute monarchy, although it may never be described as "Christo-monism." He is Lord "to the glory of God the Father," and His Lordship is presented in our midst through the work of the Holy Spirit.

Fourthly, the finality of Christ indicates the all-inclusiveness of His Lordship. It encompasses the whole world and the whole man. It covers the whole of our life. He is the beginning and the end, both of the creation and of the "new creation"; He is not simply one's personal Saviour, but a cosmic Christ whose pre-existence as well as proexistence holds all things together for good.

Fifthly, the finality of Christ means that in the man Jesus, in His faith, in His active and passive obedience, in His love toward the Father and His fellow men, we can discern the final depth and completeness of "mature manhood." He is the "be-all" and the "end-all" of our existence, the exemplary destination of us all.

Sixthly, we must emphasize that the finality of Christ is a "strange" one.[1] For He is Lord while at the same time He is our servant. His Lordship is a Lordship of suffering love; His finality is the finality of the cross and the resurrection, a finality which leads through death to life, through self-giving and self-sacrifice to ultimate vic-

---

[1] Cf. Paul Verghese, "The Finality of Jesus Christ in the Age of Universal History" in *Ecumenical Review*, Vol. XV, No. 1, October 1962, p. 25.

tory. "The Cross of Christ is both the sign of God's grace, and of conquest over the opposing powers and spirits. The Crucified is the Victor."[2]

Seventhly, the finality of Christ means God's solidarity with the world, for in Christ's incarnation and crucifixion, God, in His own unique way, identified Himself with the estranged creation and manifested the continuity of His love and care for the whole world. At the same time Christ's finality, as revealed in His resurrection and ascension, demonstrates that God's holy love is more powerful than sin. It is victor over it and effects a marvelous discontinuity in the universal history. It is the breaking of His Kingdom into this world and the beginning of the Messianic age.

Lastly, the finality of Christ contains both fulfillment and expectancy, the elements of both revelation and hiddenness, causing a tension between the "already" and the "not-yet," and resolving it again and again in the experience of the redemptive "now." He who believes in the finality of salvation promised and brought forth by Christ is raised by His power to a new life here and now and "begins in this life the eternal Sabbath."[3]

CERTAINTY AND LOVE

Just as Christ's fullness and His freedom have important bearings upon the nature and the mission of the Church, so does His finality. We mention here only two.

The first is an indestructible *certainty* that is breathed into all the concerns and undertakings of the Church. Wilhelm Andersen speaks of this in unforgettable words:

[2] Hartenstein, *Mission zwischen gestern und morgen*, p. 61. Quoted by Wilhelm Andersen, *Towards a Theology of Mission*, SCM Press, London, 1955, p. 42.

[3] *Heidelberg Catechism*, Question 103.

Through the incarnation, crucifixion, and resurrection of Jesus Christ God has created realities in the course of this world which are *immovable*. After God followed the sending of His Son with the sending of His Holy Spirit, He began with the founding of the Church to free and claim men for His coming Kingdom. *Therefore* all the mission work of the Church lives in a *certainty* which can be shaken neither by human omission nor guilt, neither by any earthly failure: He will gloriously carry out His work.[4]

The second is rooted and grounded in the fact that the one holy catholic Church derives its being from God's universal love for the whole world. And if it is true that "the world is God's first love, His first fiancée,"[5] and not the Church; if it is also true that "God is the great 'extrovert' who has turned Himself out toward man in relentless love"[6] (and that means that He turned toward all men in all the world), then the Church also, as the ministerial and missionary Body of Jesus Christ, must again and again overcome all the temptations of a self-centered introversion, must make God's concern for the world its own concern and find its destination in the dimension of breadth, that is, in the imitation of God's holy love. And only a Church which is recaptured again and again by the finality of Christ, in the sense of His exclusiveness both as the Saviour and as the Lord of the world, will be able to live the life of an all-inclusive

---

[4] Wilhelm Andersen, "Further Towards a Theology of Mission" in *The Theology of the Christian Mission*, edited by Gerald H. Anderson, McGraw-Hill Book Company, New York, 1961, p. 303; italics added.

[5] Hans-Ruedi Weber, *Salty Christians*, The Seabury Press, New York, 1963, p. 10.

[6] Donald G. Miller, "Pauline Motives for the Christian Mission" in *The Theology of the Christian Mission*, edited by G. H. Anderson, pp. 78-79.

love and spell out the spirit of true catholicity in the deepest sense of God's evangel: "God so loved the *world* that he gave his only Son." Therefore, "go and make disciples of *all nations*" by loving and serving them, not only in word or speech but in *deed* and in *truth*.

THE DIMENSION OF BREADTH

In the previous chapters we pointed out the "fullness" and the "freedom" of Christ and showed that the two should never be separated from each other. The former mobilizes the dimension of height in the life of our faith and demands from the Church daily obedience. The latter brings into motion the dimension of length, eliciting in us both gratitude and hope. This is the place to emphasize that the "fullness" and the "freedom" of Christ are held together by His "finality," and that it is this finality that gives birth within the faith of the Church to the dimension of breadth. This again serves as the matrix for "the greatest thing in the world," called love. The Church is blessed with the enriching experience of true catholicity only if in its encounter with the world it rediscovers each day that the expansion of its faith is possible only through the works of love. For in Christ Jesus only one thing counts, namely, faith in His finality as it expresses itself in love (Gal. 5:6).

This love, however, is not simply any kind of love.[7] It should not be confused with *eros*-love, which may bring forth only a fleeting union between the opposite sexes nor should it be limited to *storgē*-love, which furnishes the climate for the smallest possible social unit, the family; neither should it be identified with *philia*-love, the matrix

[7] For a more elaborate discussion of the various patterns of love see William Barclay, "*Agapē* and *Agapan*: The Greatest of the Virtues," in *More New Testament Words*, Harper, 1958, pp. 11-24; and the author's book, *Light Against Darkness*, pp. 98-102.

of tender, personal affections, for the essence of this lies definitely in the limiting principles of preferences. The love which alone can give breadth to our catholic faith is *agapē*-love, which is the gift of God's grace, the product of the Spirit, and the result of a new birth. Yet this is the only love that must be insisted upon. In fact, it is this kind of love that is again and again commanded in the gospel message. All the other patterns of love are experienced primarily as emotional affairs; they simply happen to us. We cannot help falling in love or loving our kith and kin. We cannot help liking the personal qualities of our most intimate friends. *Agapē*-love, however, differs from all others by being a responsible decision; it is the act of a principled mind and of a victorious, overcoming will.

The principle involved in *agapē*-love is that of sacrificial living and sacrificial giving. This principle is revealed and exemplified in God's love for us. "The love of Christ controls us!" exclaimed Paul (II Cor. 5:14a), and he meant primarily Christ's love for the whole world, and for each one of us individually. Christ's *agapē*-love always precedes our own. Ours is only a response to His, a reciprocating love, an act of double identification, an obedient love to Him and His holiness, and a compassionate, outgoing love toward a broken, unrestored world. For "he who has known God's loving concern for his own brokenness must share that concern for a broken world." And "he who has known the joy of membership in the people of God is obligated to seek to extend the bounds of God's people until they take in every life in every land."[8] *Agapē*-love is indeed the mainspring of the Church's missionary concern and enterprise.

[8] Donald G. Miller, *The Nature and Mission of the Church,* John Knox Press, Richmond, Va., 1957, p. 39.

The motivating force of this undertaking is the conviction that, irrespective of their race, color, class, or status, Christ died for all men. He died for all because He sympathized with all. He "was and is the Master Fellow-traveller and we cannot afford to be less. He was and is the 'all-symp,' and we have to share in His universal sympathy."[9] A truly evangelical and truly catholic Church must regard all men as "brothers for whom Christ died." And it cannot think and act as though Christ had sacrificed His life only for church members and not for all men. In other words, it will take the whole *oikumenē* (the entire inhabited earth) as its mission field. *The Wide World, My Parish* is the title of a recent book by Yves Congar, a Roman Catholic. It only re-echoes the well-known statement by John Wesley "I look upon the world as my parish." At this place we do well to remind ourselves that the English word "parish" etymologically points back to the Greek word *paroikia*, meaning "sojourning in a strange land" (cf. Acts 13:17; I Pet. 1:17). And so we might say that the Church as a "parish" would certainly perish (i.e., lose its *raison d'être*, its essential nature and destiny) if it did not let itself be motivated by a compassionate, outgoing love for all the citizens of a sadly estranged world.

THE WRATH AND THE JUDGMENT OF GOD

Two more things need to be said about *agapē*-love as the dimension of breadth in our missionary faith. The first is that its sacrificial principle as exemplified in Christ's dying for us has a disciplinary effect upon the life of the Church and through it on the life of the whole world. God's *agapē*-love is never a sentimental affair. It always contains His wrath also, and this is but His holy

[9] Paul Verghese, *op. cit.*, p. 21.

love in action against sin. "The wrath of God is revealed from heaven against all ungodliness and wickedness of men who by their wickedness suppress the truth" (Rom. 1:18). It would mean defeating God's own cause, should the Church as Christ's missionary Body withhold the proclamation of God's judgment and wrath from a world which constantly needs to be reminded of them. On the other hand, it would mean the same even in a double measure if this proclamation of God's wrath and judgment were the first or the last word of the Church to the world. For the first and the last place in the Church's missionary message surely belong to the cross of Jesus, where righteousness and peace kiss each other and the salvation of God is offered to those who fear Him. There certainly is judgment in the cross, but it is wrapped up in God's grace. And only at the foot of the cross can we become acquainted with the basic solidarity between the Church and the world. For the cross alone is "the place . . . where both the world and the Church are judged and receive forgiveness."[10]

The Church, if it is truly Evangelical and truly Catholic, knows about all this; but the world does not. And if the world cares for forgiveness at all, it would like to get it without being judged. Thus it often remains hostile toward the Church's message, and causes its *agapē*-love to assume the form of suffering.

SUFFERING: "THE TRAGIC MODE OF LEARNING"

The second important thing that needs to be said about the dimension of breadth is that it necessarily implies unjust suffering. For just as Jesus had to endure pain on

10 M. A. C. Warren, "The Christian Mission and the Cross" in *Missions under the Cross,* edited by Norman Goodall, The Friendship Press, New York, 1953, p. 26.

the cross while suffering unjustly, so the Church must time and again learn that it must share His sufferings and be a "Church under the Cross" (cf. I Pet. 2:19-25; Phil. 3:10). The present social revolution in the United States, indeed in the whole world, certainly offers the Church plenty of opportunity to learn this lesson. Verghese aptly calls this suffering love "the tragic mode of learning," "the method of identification and involvement, of suffering with and for the world, in order that we may learn wisdom."[11] And a group of theologians and missionaries, reflecting upon the missionary task of the Church, has rightly drawn the following conclusion: "In the last resort, the Church's strength lies in suffering endured with hope, and prayer offered in persevering love."[12]

APOSTOLIC MISSION AND MINISTRY

The dimension of breadth, as the area for sacrificial love, should never be viewed isolated from the other dimensions of our catholic faith. For it originates together with them and constantly converges with them. And as the Church's obedience to the fullness of Christ, as well as its gratitude for His free self-giving in the past and its hope for it for the future, meet with the Church's unreserved response to the "finality" of Christ in the form of its compassionate love toward the whole world, the spontaneous and outgoing miracle happens again and again: the apostolic succession is being translated into the apostolic mission and ministry of the whole Church. There is no apostolic mission without apostolic succession. But the reverse is equally true: without the apostolic mission and ministry of the Church its apostolic succession

11 *Op. cit.*, pp. 22, 24.
12 *The Missionary Task of the Church: Theological Reflections*, Division of Studies, World Council of Churches, Vol. VII, No. 2, (1961), p. 8.

suffers and becomes the victim of self-centered introversion. The nature and destiny of the Church can certainly not be fully grasped without an experimental dis-
cernment of the spontaneous togetherness and reciprocity
between the two.

T. W. Manson, seeing how the concept of "apostolic
succession" has been repeatedly misinterpreted in an un-
biblical way, at one point raised the question, "Would it
not be a good thing to dispense with the misleading term
'apostolic succession,' which carries with it the idea that
someone has died and left his rights and property to someone else?"[13] In the preceding chapters we certainly did
not dispense with it. For we are not of the opinion that
simply because an otherwise appropriate term has been
abused and misinterpreted, it should be dropped altogether. Rather, it should be vindicated by a right interpretation and appropriate use.

"Apostolic succession," in its true biblical sense, and as
we interpreted it, means the following of the apostles in
their teaching of, and living in, the gospel. It is a whole-
Church movement, an unbroken spiritual chain of witness-
bearing, a succession of the faithful and their service. It
is not possible simply to stand in it; the Church must
always walk in it, work in it, and serve in it. And only
thus can the Church also grow in it.

At this juncture it must be pointed out that as soon
as this apostolic succession is narrowed down to the
"historic succession" of certain officeholders in the Church
the temptation becomes great to change it from a movement to a status, from a dynamic growth to stagnation.
"Standing" in the apostolic succession and self-congratulatory ecclesiastical introversion then mean practically
one and the same thing.

---

[13] T. W. Manson, *The Church's Ministry*, Westminster Press, Philadelphia, 1948, p. 58.

The biblical concept of the apostolate, however, is exactly the opposite. For it strives only in the dimension of breadth, in the activating climate of outgoing love, in the act of overcoming all kinds of self-centeredness — even that of ecclesiastical introversion. The apostolate is a *sine qua non* for the nature and the mission of the Church, and by viewing it as only one of many functions of the Church we certainly degrade it to a subordinate and, for that reason, inappropriate role.

THE CHURCH: A FUNCTION OF THE APOSTOLATE

J. C. Hoekendijk, the Dutch missionary-theologian, in his various writings does not cease to emphasize that the apostolate is not a function of the Church, but that the Church is a function of the apostolate.

> It is common to think . . . of the apostolate, as a function of the Church. *Credo ecclesiam apostolicam* is often interpreted as: "I believe in the Church, which has an apostolic function." Would it not be truer to make a complete turn-over here, and to say what this means: I believe in the Church, which is a function of the apostolate, that is, an instrument of God's redemptive action in this world. . . . The Church is (nothing more, but also nothing less!) a means in God's hand to establish *shalom* (peace, salvation) in this world. It is taken into the triumphal procession of the glorified Son of Man and on its way it discovers that it walks amid the tokens of the coming Kingdom.[14]

Karl Barth speaks in the same vein when he points out that the adjective "apostolic" (*apostolica*) does not say anything new in relation to the three definitions of the

---

[14] J. C. Hoekendijk, "The Call to Evangelism," in *The International Review of Missions*, Vol. XXXIX, No. 154 (April, 1950) , p. 170. See also his article "Christ and the World in the Modern Age" in *Student World*, 1961, Nos. 1-2.

oneness (*una*), holiness (*sancta*) and catholicity (*catholica*) of the Church (*ecclesia*), "but it describes with remarkable precision the *concrete spiritual criterion* which enables us to answer the question whether and to what extent, in this or that case, we have or have not to do with the one, holy, catholic Church."[15] The apostolate is the spiritual criterion that urges the Church to live and to work "in the discipleship, in the school, under the normative authority, instruction, and direction of the apostles." And it is a *concrete* criterion that ushers in "the being of the community as an event" and helps to incite each member of the Church to participate in the movement of apostolic succession and ministry. All this is, of course, the work of the Holy Spirit and can therefore be known only to those who live in the act of faith.

Which are the basic principles of this apostolate?

THE TRIUNE GOD AS ABSOLUTE SUBJECT

The first basic principle is that the Triune God is the center of the apostolate. It is God the Father, in Jesus Christ, and through the Holy Spirit, who is the originating and absolute Subject of the Church's apostolic mission and ministry. For God in Christ and through the Holy Spirit not only constitutes, convokes, and confirms the Church, but He also causes the Church to come of age and *commissions* it to participate in His work of restoring the world. Again, in Christ and through the Holy Spirit, God exercises His control over the Church not only in helping it to commune with Him, to congregate in Him, and to be conformed to Him, but also in placing it continually in concrete life situations, that is, in an estranged and hostile world, so that it may have the opportunity and the task to become a *confessing* Church.

[15] Karl Barth, *Church Dogmatics*, Vol. IV, 1, pp. 712-715.

THE CHURCH COMING TO ITSELF

The second basic principle of the apostolate is that the nature of the Church is dynamic. "The Church has no fixed place," writes Hoekendijk. "It *happens* in so far as it actually proclaims the Kingdom to the world. The Church has no other existence than *in actu Christi,* that is, *in actu Apostoli.*"[16] Thus the works of evangelism and missionary activity are the very manifestations of its real nature. "Evangelism," stated the Evanston Assembly, "is no specialized or separable or periodic activity, but is rather a dimension of the total activity of the Church . . . . [It is] the place where the Church discovers itself in its true depth and outreach."[17] The German Hartenstein said something similar about the missionary work of the Church. "The missionary enterprise reveals the deepest meaning of the Church as that Body which is sent by God, as the new humanity, as the first fruits of redemption. It is impossible to speak rightly of the Church, without speaking of its mission to the world. The Church exists in its missionary activity."[18] Another Dutch missionary-theologian, Johannes Blauw, expresses the same thing in one concise sentence: "It is exactly by going outside itself that the Church *is* itself and comes to itself."[19] For the same reason the Swiss Hans-Ruedi Weber emphasizes that "the Church lives not only in assembly, but in dispersion too . . . , " and "in our 'interim time, the 'normal' form of existence of the Church is the *diaspora.* . . . What happens

16 J. C. Hoekendijk, "The Church in Missionary Thinking," in *The International Review of Missions,* Vol. XLI, No. 163 (1952), p. 334.

17 *Evangelism — The Mission of the Church to Those Outside Her Life* (Report of Section II).

18 Hartenstein, *Mission zwischen gestern und morgen,* p. 19 (quoted by Andersen, *op. cit.,* p. 54).

19 Johannes Blaauw, *The Missionary Nature of the Church,* McGraw Hill Book Company, New York, 1962, p. 122.

in the small circle of the congregation gathered for worship must also be a preparation for the role of the 'salt of the earth' which is that of the larger, concentric circle of the Church in everyday life. We come together in order to go apart."[20] He calls our attention to the biblical rhythm of the Church's withdrawal from the world (the Church in its *gathered* phase) and its return to it (the Church in its *scattered* phase). As members of the Church, we must rediscover and live in the same rhythm; otherwise "we shall never become the worshipping and ministering community the world so badly needs."[21]

TAKING THE WORLD SERIOUSLY

The third basic principle of the Apostolate is that the world must be seen in a new light.

If God in Christ's incarnation and atonement has shown once for all that He takes the world, even in its estranged condition, seriously, and that He continuously reclaims it for Himself, then the Church must do the same. It must constantly undergo a double conversion, namely, a conversion from the world to Christ and a conversion to the service with Christ in the world — to *"holy worldliness."*[22] "We shall not meet with Christ," writes J. E. Lesslie Newbigin, "except by going right into the world, into the very situations where it appears that Christ is being denied."[23]

"At the edge of the Church and the world" (H. R. Weber) there certainly is no time for theologizing about the "fullness of the Church," and whether it is or is not

---

[20] Hans-Ruedi Weber, "The Marks of an Evangelizing Church" in *The Missionary Church in East and West*, edited by Charles C. West and David M. Paton, SCM Press, London, 1959, pp. 109-110.

[21] Hans-Ruedi Weber, *Salty Christians*, pp. 4, 14.

[22] Cf. Hans-Ruedi Weber, *op cit.*, p. 49.

[23] J. E. Lesslie Newbigin, "The Gathering up of History into Christ" in *The Missionary Church in East and West*, p. 88.

conditioned by the so-called "historic episcopate." Rather, in frontier situations the Church is challenged to develop new, flexible forms of ministries.[24] Perhaps it will have to ordain a man with pastoral gifts, even if he continues to work in a secular employment. Or it may have to send certain selected ministers into secular employments so that by becoming a part of the community they may be able to bear witness to Christ more effectively. In certain other situations "team ministries" may be needed to cross denominational lines; or "itinerant ministers" who can respond effectively to rapidly changing conditions. Such a flexibility in bringing forth new forms of ministries would certainly be the best and most effective sign that the Church regards its mission to the world the summons of Christ's finality both as the Saviour and the Lord of the world.

URGENCY, UNITY AND MISSION

The final basic principle of the apostolate is that of urgency. This urgency also links together the unity and the mission of the Church.

We live in "the last hour" (I John 2:18), the age in which "the issue Christ-or-Antichrist is going to be pressed harder and harder upon the conscience of every man."[25] There is no time left for detouring around the burning issues of our days. More and more we are urged to discern "the signs of the times," namely, that the end of the earth and the end of time are joined together in their eschatological setting; that a "world community . . . is pressing upon us in its secular form every day,"[26] and that the unity

[24] Cf. what follows with Section III of the Report of the Fourth World Conference on Faith and Order, Montreal, 1963, entitled, *The Redemptive Work of Christ and the Ministry of His Church.*
[25] J. E. Lesslie Newbigin, *op. cit.,* p. 88.
[26] *Ibid.,* p. 90.

of the world in God's creation and salvation demands that our divided churches examine and re-examine the oneness of their apostolic mission. If not in their assemblies, then at least in their dispersion, if not in the gathered phase, then at least in the scattered phase, our churches must learn that unity is urgently needed for the the mission of the Church, and that the mission of the Church has for its objective the *anakephalaiosis* of the whole world, the uniting of all things in Him (Eph. 1:10) whose fullness, freedom, and finality have no end.

BEACHHEAD AND BRIDGE

It is stated of the child Jesus that He was "set for a sign that is spoken against" (Luke 2:34). And the Letter to the Hebrews refers to the mature Jesus as "the pioneer and perfecter of our faith" who patiently and courageously endured the hostility of sinners (12:2-3). He lived in constant tension with the world, yet sacrificed His life for it. By judging it He saves it (John 9:39; 12:47). And His atoning death on the cross proved that God's attitude toward a sinful world is not a sort of "kindly judgment" nor a "good-natured indulgence" but that of "consuming fire" and "costly reconciliation."[27] Jesus lived a life of "holy nonconformity," yet He was also "the good shepherd" who laid down His life for the sheep. His *diakonia* was both a ministry of holy maladjustment and a ministry of reconciliation.

The Church, as the ministerial and missionary Body of Christ, in endeavoring to fulfill its apostolate, must follow in His steps. The dichotomy of God's Word, its invitational ("Come unto me . . .") as well as its disciplining ("Woe unto you . . . ") character, and the fact that its pro-

[27] For an excellent discussion of this subject see D. M. Baillie, *God Was in Christ,* Scribner's, New York, 1948, pp. 171-179.

testations contain the elements of both negation and affirmation — all these oblige the Church to regard its mission, just as Jesus did His own, as a ministry of both rebuke and reconciliation. We may describe this twofold requirement by stating that the apostolic Church, in discharging its ministry, must serve both as a *beachhead* and as a *bridge*.[28]

The beachhead Church is always on the offensive, not willing to enter into fellowship with darkness (Eph. 6:14). It discharges the mission of the prophetic critic and constrains its members to bear witness to the exclusiveness of the gospel truth. It is the Church Militant which abhors appeasement or peace at any price, demands repentance and obedience to God, and testifies to the divine imperative. It conveys the message of righteousness by challenging the conscience of individuals, states, and societies, and moves as a "mighty army" "wholly geared to conquest," always ready to confront the world with the threatenings of God's judgment. It is the unwelcome Church, the *ecclesia non grata,* the society of outspoken men, and the fortress of those who are hated, persecuted, and even put to death for Christ's sake. Its witness is motivated by a faith that rebels, and it brings upon itself the well-known indictment: "These men who have turned the world upside down have come here also" (Acts 17:6). Finally, the beachhead Church is an uncompromising Church, never willing to promote the cause of political power blocks, nor to be an accomplice in unjustified social and political revolutions or among those who selfishly or complacently wish to preserve the *status quo.*

The bridge Church, on the other hand, is always ready to identify itself with the world, to become all things to

[28] For a more elaborate discussion of what follows see the author's book, *Light Against Darkness,* pp. 112-115.

142

all men so that it may by all means save some. It enjoins its members always to speak and to do the truth in the spirit 'of a compassionate, inclusive love (Eph. 4:15), and fulfills a communal, integrating mission. It offers to all, whether they accept or reject it, the forgiveness of God; testifies to His grand indicative; comforts all men in their state of existential predicament, and testifies that Christ's Church is the fellowship of forgiven and forgiving sinners who are always seeking to recapture the world with tokens of His mercy, who are always ready to heal the sick, to find the lost, and to liberate men from the prison-house of their sins and alienation. It is the community of silently forbearing men who are willing to share in His sufferings (Phil. 3:10) and with an outgoing, compassionate love "to hold the world together." Finally, the bridge Church remains under all circumstances "the Church with open doors and large windows" (Barth), an inclusive community ready to outhope all justified revolutions and to outlove both the radicals and the conservatives.

ONE AND THE SAME CHURCH

To all this we hasten to add that the beachhead Church and the bridge Church are not two different churches but consistently and unchangeably one and the same Church; and the ministry of rebuke and reconciliation are not two separate ministries that contradict or oppose each other but two interlocking, dynamic aspects of the Church's one apostolic ministry. Only a Church which discharges both will be able to remain "a new and continually renewed community with God (sacred, not sacral); looking toward the world (secular, not secularist) in a life distinguished, but not isolated, from the world (spiritual, not spiritualist) ."[29] Only such a Church will live up to the demands of God's ultimate purpose and of its own ultimate concern, grow steadily in its apostolic succession and mission, and prove itself, not only in words but also in deeds, a truly evangelical, truly catholic, and truly reformed Church.

[29] J. Blauw, "The Mission of the People of God," in *The Missionary Church in East and West*, p. 100.

CHAPTER EIGHT:

Constant Contrition and Ever New Commitments

The United Church will be truly evangelical, truly catholic, and truly reformed if, while working for the restoration of the whole world, it remains at the same time conscious of the necessity of its own up-building and renewal. For that reason the depth of our faith must be determined by the faithfulness of Christ as it demands from the Church constant contrition and ever new commitments. And as the depth of our faith meets with the height, the length, and the breadth of it, the movement of the Church's renewal is spelled out in a continuous reformation. That in turn means that our witnessing (or pro-testing) to God's faithfulness in Christ and through the Holy Spirit must always be coupled with courage and readiness to begin the work of reformation in

> *the Church itself. But such a courage and such a*
> *readiness are possible only as gifts of a faithful God.*
> *Therefore a truly evangelical, truly catholic, and*
> *truly reformed Church shall never cease to pray:*
> "Veni Creator Spiritus! *Thou who hast* formed
> *Thy Church, wilt Thou* reform *it again and again!"*

The gist of the seven preceding chapters may best be indicated by combining a confession of St. Augustine with a partly paraphrased exclamation of John Wesley referred to before: "I take the whole Christ for my Saviour, the whole Bible for my staff, the whole Church for my fellowship, and the whole world for my parish."

However, one final question still remains to be settled: Am *I* — or, better, are *we* as members of the Church qualified in ourselves for such a tremendous undertaking? *Can* we, or rather, *dare* we claim anything as our own? Both the Word of God (cf. II Cor. 3:4-6) and our own deepest Christian experience teach us that whatever qualifications we may have, they all come from the Spirit of God. The Church and we as its members do not simply possess our own being, for the reality of the Church as well as our so-called "established membership" in it are rooted and grounded in the dynamic interlocking of two irreversible events, namely, (1) Christ's constant *coming* to us, and (2) (with His help) our constant *overcoming* of ourselves and the world in which we live or, in other words, the Church's continuous *upbuilding,* which is initiated, demanded, and achieved by a faithful God, yet never without our own *renewal.*

UPBUILDING AND RENEWAL

In Acts 9:31 we read a joyous report about the spreading of the Church: how it was upheld by the Spirit; how it grew in numbers throughout Judea, Galilee and Samaria; and how it was *built up*. Then, later on, in the fifteenth chapter we are told about the conference at Jerusalem and how jubilant the apostles and elders were when they first heard about God's visitation among the Gentiles. James saw in this the fulfillment of Amos 9:11-12: God was *rebuilding* the "fallen house of David" amidst the Gentiles, for they, too, were claimed as His own and moved to seek the Lord. And so the Church proved to be the Church in its missionary activity. Its apostolic ministry brought in new members and in this way helped to *build up* the Body of Christ.

But this is only one aspect of the Church's role. The other one is the pastoral aspect. For the building up of the Church in its scattered phase is made possible only through the continuous upbuilding of the Church in its gathered phase. Hence to the task of converting non-Christians must be added the task of the never ceasing "edification" of those who are already members of the Church and to the proclamation of the good news (*kerygma*), the mutual sharing in the apostles' teaching (*didachē*).

Four relevant things should be noted about this dual role of the Church's upbuilding. First of all, whether new churches are being built up or old churches "edified," *ultimately all is done by the power of the Word of God.* Paul in his farewell speech to the Ephesian elders commended them to the Word of God's grace which alone is "able *to build* [*them*] *up* and to give [them] the inheritance among all those who are sanctified" (Acts 20:32). He assures the Corinthians that his apostolic authority was given to him not to tear them down but to build them up, and that this authority resides in words taught him by the Spirit (II Cor. 10:8; I Cor. 2:13). He also admonishes them that above everything else they should prefer an edifying work that is done through intelligent prophecy (I Cor. 14:3, 6) and in the Spirit of *agapē*-love (I Cor. 8:1) .

Secondly, though the process of edification is usually a person-to-person affair, it should never be regarded a private transaction; for *its final goal is the upbuilding of the whole Church.* That was Paul's main argument in the matter of speaking in tongues. The language of ecstasy may have an edifying effect upon the speaker himself. The man who prophesies, however, speaks to all in the Church and thus "builds up a Christian community." Therefore the members of the Church should strive to excel in the use of those spiritual gifts that advance the cause of their "mutual upbuilding" or, as the Bible states it, they should "pursue the things . . . that build up the common life" (cf. I Cor. 14:4, 12; Rom. 14:9) .

Thirdly, the edification of the Church *must continually go on.* The Christian community can never settle down; it must remain constantly on the move. And at no point should it say to itself: "Zion, you have many goods laid up for many years; take life easy and enjoy yourself." For on the calendar of the Church's self-edification each day is but another commencement day. As the living house of the living God, the Church needs constant building up. *Ecclesia edificanda quia edificata.*

One more thing needs mentioning here. The secret of the Church's edification does not lie with psychological pep talks, inventive educational methods, or social activities. The church may well utilize "order and ardor," but not even these can guarantee its edification. For *the Church's genuine upbuilding is but an expression of its total renewal.* That, again, has its source in nothing less than the *faithfulness* of Christ as it demands from us (and evokes in us) constant *contrition* and ever new *commitments.* The Church can be truly evangelical, truly catholic, and truly reformed only if it lives in such a constant renewal. *Ecclesia renovanda quia renovata.*

THE FAITHFULNESS OF CHRIST

Why does God allow suffering? Why does He let evil exist at all? Such and similar questions are difficult ones even for our Christian faith. And they demand again and again a solution as we actually encounter the unpredictable contingencies of daily life.

The Heidelberg Catechism meets the problem of evil head on as it bears witness to an "Almighty God" who at the same time is also a "faithful Father." "Whatever evil He [God] sends upon me in this troubled life He will turn to my good, for He is able to do it, being Almighty God, and is willing to do it, being a faithful Father." Not "goodness," "love," or "mercy," but definitely *faithfulness* is the primary motive for God's willingness to overrule all evil occurrences. And I can count on Him because "for the sake of Christ His Son" He is "my God and my Father."[1]

The Catechism, in its very first question and answer, points also to the faithfulness of *Christ*. Our only comfort in life and in death is that we have a "faithful Saviour" and belong to Him. Again, we have in Him not merely a "good," "loving," "compassionate," or "merciful," but definitely a *faithful* Saviour, one who will never disappoint us but makes Himself always available to us.

In the preceding chapter we learned that the fullness and the freedom of Christ are held together by His finality. Now we have reached the point where we can state that all three *are made available* to us by His faithfulness. The Church's controlling power may well be the fullness of Christ, the undergirding factor of its con-

---

[1] *Heidelberg Catechism,* Question 26.

tinuity the freedom of Christ, and the driving force of its ultimate concern His finality. But it is only because of His faithfulness that the Church Militant turns into a Church Triumphant and in its constant renewal actually proves that Christ's promise to His Church is in the process of constantly being made good. Behold, not even the powers of death prevail against it!

God's faithfulness has nothing to do with the abstract, speculative ideas of timelessness and unchangeableness. It can be known only from His unique, historical revelation in Jesus Christ. "God is faithful!" exclaimed Paul. For it was by Him that we "were called into the fellowship of his Son, Jesus Christ our Lord" (I Cor. 1:9). By the threefold coming of the true Light, the newness of the new age was inaugurated. But not only that, for in the ever-recurring renewal of His Church we can discern also the ongoing work of His Spirit. And so we, too, exclaim, "God is faithful, for He is keeping the new age always and constantly new!" In Christ Jesus, and through His "guarantee," the Spirit, it is God who never ceases to feed the Church by His faithfulness.

It is God's faithfulness, in Christ and through His Spirit, that causes Him to forgive again and again the sins of the individual members, and so also the sins of the whole Church, and cleanses it from all unrighteousness (I John 1:9). It is God's faithfulness that strengthens the Church in the life of its members, and guards it from evil (II Thess. 3:3). Again, it is God's faithfulness that sanctifies the Church in its members *wholly* and keeps it sound and blameless at the coming of our Lord Jesus Christ (I Thess. 5:23-24). And, finally, it is the same faithfulness of God that will not let His Church be tempted beyond its strength but with the temptation will also provide it the way of escape (I Cor. 10:13). Even if the Church should prove to be temporarily faithless, God will always remain faithful, for He cannot deny Himself (II Tim. 2:13).

And so the Church learns again and again that the God who is faithful is also kind, forbearing and patient; that He is a long-suffering God; and by being this He alone can penetrate the depth of our being, grasp His Church at the very taproot of its existence and lead it to repentance and renewal. Nothing can pierce to the place where our "life and spirit, joints and marrow, divide," as do the words of our faithful Saviour: "Repent, for the kingdom of God is at hand" (Matt. 3:2) and, after it has repented, "Be faithful unto death" (Rev. 2:10).

And so we have arrived at the crucial point of our whole discourse. For the most relevant events in the life of a truly evangelical, truly catholic, and truly reformed Church always originate in this fourth dimension of our Christian faith — in the dimension of depth.

THE DIMENSION OF DEPTH

Our first three basic words were "control," "continuity," and "concern." Their meaningfulness unfolded itself as we tried to analyze the height, the length, and the breadth of our Christian faith and to associate with them certain attitudes, such as obedience, gratitude, hope, and love. Now, as we descend into the dimension of depth, two further basic words gain relevancy. They are "contrition" and "commitment," or "repentance" and "renewal" in the sense of sincere re-formation.

A church without a contrite heart is not even a counterfeit church. It is simply no church at all. For the birthplace of the reality of the Church is always at that point of no return where we (you and I, both in our solitariness and our togetherness) begin to despair of ourselves, acknowledge that we are in utter need of the forgiveness of our sins, take our refuge in the crucified and risen Lord, and are transformed into a fellowship of forgiven and forgiving sinners. And this point of no return will have to present itself again and again in the life of the Church, as St. Augustine so beautifully expressed:

> As long as she is here, the whole Church prays: "Forgive us our sins." Thus she is here not without spot or wrinkle, but through that, which she has received, she is brought to that glory and perfection, which does not exist here.[2]

The depth of the Church's faith can be ascertained only by sounding it with the plumb line of repentance. The more sincere the Church's repentance, the deeper its faith. Five of the seven letters written to the churches in Revelation 2 and 3 were calls to repentance. These churches were called upon to turn about, to make a complete about-face; to change their whole mind and the course of their life, to remember from what they had fallen away and to return to their first love which they had abandoned.

The same call to repentance comes to all the churches ever since. They all are certainly in desperate need of receiving such a call, for which of them could prove to be a truly evangelical, truly catholic, and truly reformed church without such repentance? Not without good reason did Luther begin his 95 Theses with the following sentence: "Our Lord and Master Jesus Christ in saying, 'Repent ye' (Matt. 4:17), wanted the entire life of believers to be repentance."

In our twentieth century, the century of the ecumenical movement, this call to repentance is at the same time a call to unity. The churches need to be reminded that

---

[2] Quoted by W. A. Visser 't Hooft, *The Renewal of the Church*, Westminster, 1956, p. 39.

ultimate unity lies in the opposite direction from where it has been sought. For in the midst of the Roman Catholic-Protestant dialogues, of the consultations on church union, and even the occasional "mergers" and "reunions," there will still be need for sincere contrition, for a complete about-face, and there will still be room left for "a penitent return to that which was originally given but subsequently denied."[3]

In the meantime, the faithfulness of God is bringing forth its new miracles in what we have called the dimension of depth. Statements are made and confessions are uttered which would not have been possible even in the first half of our century. Churches which formerly hated and cursed and anathematized, or at best shunned, each other are on the way to becoming partners in repentance. Thus, for example, we hear the Roman Catholic Hans Küng say,

> Forgive us our sins, and in particular our share in the sin of schism! . . . An honest, humble confession of this sort by the leaders of the Church today would be pleasing to our heavenly Father as few words or deeds could be; and one word of repentance would open more doors to us among our separated fellow Christians than any number of pressing invitations to return.[4]

Or let us listen to Karl Barth who could not help but close his "Thoughts on the Second Vatican Council" with self-scrutinizing words like these:

> From the one standpoint [i.e., the Roman Catholic] as from the other [i.e., the Protestant], the way of unity of the Church can only be the way of her renewal. But renewal means repentance. And repentance means turning

[3] Lesslie Newbigin, "The Nature of the Unity We Seek" in *Religion and Life,* Vol. XXVI, 1957, No. 2, p. 182.

[4] Hans Küng, *The Council, Reform and Reunion,* Sheed and Ward, 1961, p. 184.

about: not the turning of those others, but one's *own* turning. Is not the problem posed for the World Council of Churches by the Roman Council one of repentance and so of renewal of *our* churches, of all the non-Roman churches assembled in the World Council? And is not the continuation of our conversations with the others a secondary problem dominated by that primary one? This is the question . . . which seems to be the *burning* question with respect to the conclusion of the Council, and, in fact, far beyond this.[5]

The mills of a faithful God grind slow but sure. Our contrition over the divided state of the Church may not yet be sufficiently deep and constant, nevertheless, to the extent that it is the result of the grinding of the mills of a faithful God, it will bring forth new commitments. For "with God all things are possible" (Matt. 19:26).

WHEN "DEPTH" MEETS "HEIGHT"

Someone, who opposed the union between the Congregational Christian Churches and the Evangelical and Reformed Church, once made the following, rather malicious remark: "The first three capital letters, UCC, in the name of the new United Church of Christ will have to be spelled out as standing for 'Utterly Confused Christians.'" I for one like to believe that members of the United Church of Christ will prove that they want to be a fellowship of Unconditionally Committed Christians. And I delight in thinking of the forthcoming great United Church in exactly the same way.

At the same time, however, I venture to pick up even that maliciously used word "confusion" and apply it in a constructive sense. For it is not possible to form a com-

[5] Karl Barth, "Thoughts on the Second Vatican Council" in *The Ecumenical Review*, Vol. XV, 1963, No. 4, p. 367.

pany of unconditionally committed Christians *without
having first experienced the utter confusion of face in the
sight of a faithful God.* Especially when it comes to our
striving for unity, a genuine contrition of heart will
necessarily lead to the confession of our lips: "To us, O
Lord, belongs confusion of face . . . because we have sinned
against thee" (Dan. 9:8) with our divided witness which
is "indeed a scandal in the face of the non-Christian
world."[6] However, even such a confession would prove to
be but another noisy gong or clanging cymbal unless it
be followed by a complete change in our life.

Exactly here is the place to let our fifth basic word,
"commitment," stand out in bold relief. A Church that
wants to be not only truly evangelical and truly catholic,
but also truly reformed needs to undertake a thorough
analysis of the deepest meaning of Christian commitment.

The American philosopher Josiah Royce once insisted
on the practice of a "kind of loyalty to loyalty." In the
Christian Church, too, we have to foster a kind of continuing commitment to the principle of Christian commitment. However, in the life of the Church this should
never be done for the sake of the abstract principle itself
but always for the sake of Him who constitutes, convokes,
confirms, and thus also *commissions* the Church, even
Jesus Christ our Lord.

At least three things should be noted here. The first is
indicated by the title of this subsection. Christian commitments are made possible only at the point where the
"depth" of our faith meets with the "height" of it; in
other words, when our repentance does not become "arrested" but bursts into an act of new obedience. Or we
might even say, at the point where faith as a gift of God's

---

[6] *The Evanston Report,* p. 91.

grace turns into a faith that proves to be our act of over-coming.

This "point," of course, looks like a point only from a far distance. In its utmost reality, however, the meeting of the "depth" of faith with its "height" — the birth pangs of a new act of obedience in the matrix of repentance — could be best represented by a rugged line. For at such a meeting a struggle is going on between the "old age" and the "new age," between the "old humanity" and the "new humanity," between the "old Church" and the "reborn Church"; a struggle without which there could be no victory at all. Nor does such a meeting of "depth" and "height" bypass the other two dimensions of faith, name-ly, the dimensions of "length" and "breadth," for each new Christian commitment is the outcome of a magnifi-cent team work in which repentance, gratitude, hope, love, and obedience all participate. And the secret of their har-monious participation lies in the fullness, freedom, final-ity, and faithfulness of Christ.

Our second observation concerning Christian commit-ment can be stated only in a paradoxical way: There *is* such a thing, and at the same time there is *no* such thing as a once-for-all Christian commitment. Or, as Rajah B. Manikam has expressed it, "To join the Church and to remain loyal to its Lord requires one supreme act of personal surrender," but he hastened to add, "and countless daily acts of obedience to Christ."

In our own individual Christian pilgrimage as well as in the history of the Christian Church we can point at certain threshold commitments which have ushered in a new turn of spiritual events in our personal life or a new epoch in the life of the Church. On the other hand, we will have to acknowledge that not even these first and foremost commitments could have remained a power-releasing force in us, had they not found their outlet in our ever new, daily acts of obedience to Christ. Christian faith and all its dimensions are given to us and to the Church as a whole to translate them into "worldly holiness," "costly discipleship," and constantly new commitments.

The Church should never remain a defense community. It should always be on the offensive. The warfare in which it is engaged may need the sweat and work of many assemblies, many councils, many committees, subcommittees, and perhaps even sub-subcommittees. But it should never be forgotten that a committee Church is not necessarily a committed Church, and that ultimately only an ever newly committed Church can become a conquering Church.

One more thing needs to be stressed here. Only a contrite Church can be a truly committed Church; and only a truly committed Church will again and again acknowledge its need for continuous forgiveness and repentance. Therefore that concrete spiritual event in the life of the Church which we have called its apostolic succession and ministry can be visualized only as a twofold movement.

A truly evangelical, truly catholic, and truly reformed Church is always aware that its faith is constantly mingled with unbelief. For that reason its "good fight of faith" is composed of two ongoing movements. One is the movement from repentance through gratitude, hope, and love toward a faith that wants to be utter obedience. The other, equally necessary, is the movement from a never perfect act of obedience, from a well-intended yet never completed act of commitment, back to sincere contrition and thus to a faith that is acknowledged as not our own doing but always and only as the gift of God's grace. As long as the Church remains both sinful and sanctified, there will always be need for these two opposite movements. And herein definitely lies the innermost mystery of the Church's continuously ongoing reformation, the secret of its perpetual renewal — *Ecclesia reformanda quia reformata.*

COURAGE TO BE REFORMED

There is a great difference between courage to reform and courage to be reformed. The former indicates that one is bold enough to initiate an improvement or to propose certain changes which he deems necessary. Here the whole action seems to originate in the person himself and may be motivated by purely human (social, political, economic, etc.) considerations. The latter, however, points beyond the person to a movement or event he encountered before he turned into a reformer. It is only in this second, deeper sense of the word that we speak of the "reformation of the Church" and we venture to call the persons who have the courage to allow themselves to be reformed its reformers.

But something more needs to be stated here, for one can let himself be reformed by any fresh gusts of human teaching, by any cultural or religious enlightenment. Not so the reformers of the Church. Before they would even dare to participate in the reformation of the Church, they themselves first experience what it means to stand (and to walk) under the judgment (*krisis*) of God's Word. Their ideal of the Church is never simply a subjective image, a projection of wishful thinking. They believe in the corporate reality of the one, concrete, yet universal (catholic) Church which, however, is at the same time also a Church reformed according to the evangel (gospel) or, as it is more often stated, "reformed according to the Word of God." To be a reformer is to believe and to work for the Church truly evangelical, truly catholic, and truly reformed.

Here, however, we are not so much interested in the

reformers as in the reformation of the Church itself. And when we use the phrase *Ecclesia semper reformanda quia reformata,* three things are meant.

First, the Church *is* already re-formed; it *has* experienced in its own life the courage to be reformed; and this reformation originated from on high, from the gospel of Jesus Christ *(Ecclesia reformata a verbo Dei)*.

Secondly, the Church, having been re-formed, seeks its *further* reformation, and it seeks it again and again in the same Word of God *(Ecclesia reformanda a verbo Dei)*.

Thirdly, the Church is *continuously* being re-formed, as it is both a re-formed Church and a Church to be re-formed *(Ecclesia simul reformata et reformanda)*; but here again we should not neglect to add, "by the Word of God."

All this is really nothing else but the application of certain aspects of Paul's theological anthropology to the corporate reality of the Church.[7] Paul regards the Christian a "new man": "If anyone is in Christ, he *is* a new creation" (II Cor. 5:17). Yet he exhorts the same Christian man to seek his *further* renewal: "Be renewed in the spirit of your minds" (Eph. 4:23). And he speaks of him as being *continuously* renewed: "Though our outer nature is wasting away, our inner nature is being renewed every day" (II Cor. 4:16). Thus we can also say: The Church is truly reformed when it is the society of *new* men who do not cease to seek their further renewal and in seeking it are *continuously* renewed by God's Word and Spirit.

Since the reformation of the Church is such a positive, creative renewal, it should never be identified with *revolution.* The latter always aims at the more or less ruthless overthrow of values and authorities. Reformation, however, is made possible only in and through the

---

7 Cf. W. A. Visser' 't Hooft, *op. cit.,* pp. 32-36.

Church's joyous self-surrender to the eternally stable and commanding authority of the speaking God.

Nor is reformation simply *innovation*. The introducing of something novel may often mean uncritical adaptation to the current spirit of the age. The reformation of the life, doctrine, order, or ministry of the Church, on the other hand, very often finds itself struggling against the streams or winds of the various new doctrines of the age, against both the "progressives" and the "conservatives."

Reformation is much nearer to *instauration,* in the sense of restoration of the unalterable essence of the Church. Calvin did not cease to stress that the *ecclesia reformata* stood for "the restoration of the face of the ancient Catholic Church." Yet he also acknowledged that such a restoration represented only one (though a very important) aspect of the total renewal of the whole Church, and that ultimately renewal itself is God's miraculous work, nothing short of *resurrection*. "The preservation of the Church, almost every day, is accompanied with many miracles. [And so] we ought to bear in mind, that the life of the Church is not without resurrection, nay, it is not without many resurrections."[8] Could anything more exhaustive be said about the Church's reformation than this?

Father Hans Küng states: "Reformation is not a Protestant preserve."[9] He is so right! How could it be when it is God's miraculous work? He also writes: "In Catholic circles, the word 'renewal' is always preferred to the word

[8] Calvin, *Commentaries on Micah* (6:6-7). For a book which stresses "reformation" in the sense of "resurrection," with excellent further references to Calvin, see Gyula Bárczay, *Ecclesia semper reformanda, eine Untersuchung zum Kirchenbegriff des 19. Jahrhunderts.* Zurich, EVZ Verlag, 1961.

[9] *Op cit.,* p. 9. We might answer here: Nor is catholicity a preserve of the Church of Rome. If it were, it certainly would prove to be a "cabin'd, cribb'd and confined" catholicity.

'reform,' because it stresses the positive and creative aspect."[10] But why then did he in the title of the English edition of his book prefer the word "reform" to that of "renewal"? We believe that "reformation," "renewal," and "resurrection" are all equally good words. They all stress the same "positive and creative aspect," because they all indicate an event initiated, demanded, and achieved ultimately by God Himself.

The Church's resurrection is in its renewal, and its renewal is identical with its reformation.[11] And because this is so, we all can believe in a Church which is truly catholic as well as truly reformed, and which can be both of these because it is truly evangelical. May I quote here Father Küng again:

> Our most important task at the moment, on both sides [i.e., on both the Roman Catholic and the Protestant side], is reforming action within our own communion — reforming action according to the same norm, which is the Gospel of Jesus Christ.[12]

Let us hope for the time when we shall be enabled to do this reforming all together.

THE ACT OF REFORMING

Which are the characteristic traits of the act of genuine reforming? They should be practically identical with those of Christian witnessing,[13] namely, in the sense of the twofold act of protesting. In the dynamic context of the on-

10 *Op. cit.*, p. 23; cf. also p. 115.

11 It is interesting to note that while the various English translations of the New Testament render the Greek words *metaschematidzo* and *metamorphoo* with "change" (KJV, RSV), "transfigure" (EB), "remake," "remold" (Philips), and "transform" (Moffat, KJV, RSV), the Vulgate uses the words *reformabit, reformamini* (Phil. 3: 21; Rom. 12:2). Cf. Hans Küng, *op. cit.*, p. 10.

12 *Op. cit.*, p. 59.

13 Cf. the author's book, *Light Against Darkness*, pp. 126-129.

going reformation of the Church each Christian is a po-
tential reformer by virtue of the fact that he is a protesting catholic. We mention eight essential elements that
contribute to the act of genuine Christian reforming.

Necessity. By this we mean the sense of a holy in-
evitability (cf. I Cor. 9:16b; Acts 4:20). "Here I stand,
I cannot do otherwise," were the closing words of Martin
Luther at Worms. And he happened to be a Reformer.

Polarity. By this we mean putting in practice the principle of full-fledged protesting — a firm attestation to the
reforming Word and Spirit, coupled with an equally reso-
lute attack on all the idols of deformity.

Persistency. A true reformer never loses his sense of urgency. He will be ready and on hand at all times, "in
season and out of season" (II Tim. 4:2). And he will
regard each moment as an opportune time (*kairos*) of
reformation.

Intrepidity. That is, courage to accept the loss of face in
the sight of the Lord, courage to deny one's self for His
sake, and courage to speak up for *His* reforming cause.
A reformer can always confidently say:

> *The Lord is my helper,*
> *I will not be afraid;*
> *What can man do to me?* (Heb. 13:6).

Solidarity. A true reformer identifies himself with the
whole Church as the Body of Christ and with the *whole*
world for which He died. Compassionate love for the
whole man and for *all* men is the hallmark of each reforming act.

Integrity. Without integrity even this hallmark of solidarity would easily fade away. Discrepancies between
words and deeds can rob an otherwise "restored" Church
of its reforming power. The world will not listen to it,

saying, "The acts of your *koinonia* speak so loudly that we cannot hear the words of your *kerygma*."[14]

Eternity. There can be no genuine reformation without the eschatological reference. That is what keeps reformation steadily on the go. Through each reforming act that occurs between the ascension and return of Christ eternity breaks into our time. The life span of the reforming Church consists of countless redemptive "nows" as it dispenses both His judgment and His mercy.

Last, but not least, *humility*. Calvin regarded it "the sovereign virtue . . . the mother and root of all virtues." He liked to quote St. Augustine: "If you ask me concerning the precepts of the Christian religion, first, second, third and always I would answer, 'Humility.' "[15]

The act of genuine reforming must breathe humility. The same also holds true of our struggle for church union. The one great Church we hope for will come true only in that final ecumenical act of reforming which overcomes all church pride, all well-hidden, self-congratulatory attitudes, and all last residues of a false humility, a humility which is self-gratifyingly aware of its own existence.

The participants in such an ultimate reforming act will certainly not say: "All of us have won and we all have prizes."[16] Even less will any of them boast: "The prize has been won by my church; the others received but 'consolation prizes.' "[17] Nor will there be room left for such a statement as this: "We all took prizes but none of us has

14 J. C. Hoekendijk, "The Call to Evangelism" in *The International Review of Missions,* Vol. XXXIX, April 1950, p. 125.

15 John Calvin, *Sermons on Job* LXXX, and Institutes, II, 2, ii (McNeill edition, Westminster, 268-269) .

16 Cf. B. H. Streeter, *The Primitive Church,* Macmillan, 1929, p. IX.

17 Cf. W. Norman Pittenger, *The Church, the Ministry, and Reunion,* Seabury Press, 1957, p. 67.

won," especially when it is followed by a self-assuring assertion like, "My church was both catholic and reformed; thus its contributions are many."[18] Least of all will any of them say: "We had no prize at all, but when it comes to humility, we sure 'licked' all the other churches."[19]

No, the participants of that final reforming act will join in making but one great confession, voiced so humbly and beautifully centuries ago by St. Augustine:

> Out of some depth or other of God's Judgments, which we can not fathom, . . . comes forth all that we can do . . . . We see what we can do; we do not see whence we can do it — except that we see this far: that . . . it is of God.[20]

VENI CREATOR SPIRITUS!

Will there be a reunion? Are we going to be gathered into one Church, a Church truly evangelical, truly catholic, and truly reformed? Certainly not without a daily, sincere entreaty, "Come, Creator Spirit!"

In the eighteenth century, David Hollaz felt it a spiritual necessity to turn his treatment of each Christian doctrine into a prayerful sigh (a *suspirium*); to let his "language about God . . . pass expressly into language to God."[21] At the end of our discourse on church union we

[18] Cf. H. W. Montefiore, "The Historic Episcopate" in *The Historic Episcopate in the Fullness of the Church,* ed. by Kenneth M. Carey, Dacre Press, 1954, p. 126.

[19] Here I am paraphrasing a good-humored remark heard from members of a certain denomination known for its plainness: "We have neither an elaborate liturgy, nor a complicated theology, but when it comes to humility, we can lick the world."

[20] St. Augustine, *Sermons* CXXXI. 2, 3; CLXV. 5, quoted by John Calvin, *Institutes,* III, 2, 35 (McNeill edition, Westminster, I, 583). Quoted here slightly paraphrased; the plural pronoun "we" is used while Augustine uses the singular pronoun "I."

[21] Karl Barth, *Church Dogmatics,* I, 1, Scribner's, 1936, p. 25.

feel prompted to do the same thing. Could there be a
better summation of all that we have said than our turning to God with a prayer for unity which is of Him alone?
So, let us pray:

Eternal God,
Father of our Lord Jesus Christ
and our Father!
Hear us as we pray for Thy Church—
for its life, unity, and
mission to the world.

We thank thee that
in the fullness of time
Thou hast made Thy Son, Jesus Christ,
our personal Saviour,
the Head of the Church,
and the Lord of the world.

We thank Thee that in Him
Thou hast called us
to be members of the Church,
which is His Body,
and that we are
convicted and confirmed,
comforted and counseled,
controlled and commissioned
by Him alone.

We beseech Thee, O Lord,
have mercy upon us!
We all have sinned against Thee
through our shameful divisiveness.

Expose us always to Thy judgment.
Restore us always by Thy mercy.

Gather us, Lord, or scatter us;
do as Thou deemest right,
building us all into one Church:
a Church with open doors and large windows,
a Church that takes the world seriously,
ready to work and to suffer,
and even to bleed for it.

O come, Creator Spirit,
and give Thy Church the courage
always to be truly evangelical,
truly catholic, and
truly reformed.

Thou, who hast formed Thy Church,
come, and reform it again and anew.

For the sake of Christ
who is with us and prays with us
That we may all be one.

Amen.

INDEX OF SUBJECTS

INDEX OF NAMES

170

INDEX OF BIBLICAL REFERENCES